Flora Thompson

The cottage where Flora Thompson was born

Flora Thompson

The Story of the *Lark Rise* Writer

GILLIAN LINDSAY

ROBERT HALE · LONDON

© *Gillian Lindsay 1990*
First published in Great Britain 1990

Robert Hale Limited
Clerkenwell House
Clerkenwell Green
London EC1R 0HT

British Library Cataloguing in Publication Data

Lindsay, Gillian
Flora Thompson: the story of the Lark Rise Writer.
1. Fiction in English. Thompson, Flora, 1876–1947
I. Title
823'.912

ISBN 0–7090–4012–1

1 0 0 8 2 9 8 7 5

Photoset in Ehrhardt by
Derek Doyle & Associates, Mold, Clwyd.
Printed in Great Britain by
St Edmundsbury Press, Bury St Edmunds, Suffolk.
Bound by WBC Bookbinders Limited.

Contents

Illustrations

PICTURE CREDITS

Oxfordshire Photographic Archive, DLA, County Museum, Woodstock: 1–5. Banbury Museum: 6. Leslie Castle: 7. Norman Phillips: 8–9. David Lindsay: 10–11, 16. Anthony Humble Smith: 13. The Royal College of Physicians: 14. Oxford University Press: 15.

Frontispiece: Line drawing by Lynton Lamb from *Lark Rise*, 1939.
Chapter head illustrations: Wood engravings by Julie Neild Gooch from *Lark Rise to Candleford*, 1945. Reproduced by permission of Oxford University Press.

Acknowledgements

The outlines of Flora Thompson's life were drawn by Margaret Lane in her biographical essay first published in 1947: I have filled in the details. In so doing I have met the few people who still remember Flora Thompson and I have corresponded with many who, as lovers of her work, have willingly given their time to help compile this book. To all who have helped in any way I now give my grateful thanks.

First to my husband David, whose patience, interest and technical assistance has ensured that the work has been a shared pleasure, to my father for his encouragement and to my children for their tolerance.

Special thanks go to Flora Thompson's nephew, Mr Leslie Castle, for his kindness and for access to his personal collection.

To Mrs Elizabeth Murray for her unfailing enthusiasm and help with research. To Mrs Anne Mallinson of The Selborne Bookshop for her kind collaboration and support. To Mrs Eileen Hobson and Mr Joe Leggett for their memories of Flora and to Mr Norman Phillips for his memories and the two photographs of Flora with her children.

To the staffs of the libraries in Bournemouth, Winchester, Oxford and Torquay and to the County Record Offices of Hampshire, Oxfordshire and Devon. Also to Oxfordshire Museums Services.

To Mr S. Bowen of Post Office Archives in London. To the Editors of the *Bournemouth Echo*, the *Bicester Advertiser* and the *Isle of Wight County Press*.

I should also like to thank Mrs Margaret Allen, Mr L. Batten, Mrs Vera Cumberlege, Mr Patrick Cumberlege, Mr Laurence Giles, Mrs Julie Neild Gooch, Mrs G. Harrington, Mr and Mrs A. Humble-Smith, Mrs P. Massingham, Mrs Irene Northan, Mr David Ryan, Mr Alastair Souttar, Mrs Enid Silsbury, Mrs Betty Tettmar, Mr Richard Tylor, Revd G. de Burgh Thomas, Revd M. Bowles, Revd Ron Jennison.

For permission to quote from Flora Thompson's books I am grateful to her grandaughter Mrs Elizabeth Swaffield; and for the use of papers in the Flora Thompson collection. I acknowledge the help of the staff of the Harry Ransome Humanities Research Center, The University of Texas at Austin.

1 Daughter of the Hamlet

On fine afternoons in the early 1880s, a young woman called Emma Timms often took her children for walks along the turnpike road close to their hamlet home. Her son Edwin was safely strapped into the black wickerwork baby carriage which was one of her most cherished possessions, but her small daughter Flora was allowed to run free, exploring the hedgerows and roadside dells. The road joined the distant city of Oxford with Northampton, although little traffic travelled along the route of their walk. Occasionally the family saw the doctor's gig pass or a horse-drawn tradesman's van go by, but usually the road was deserted for hours on end.

The grass verges, wide as small meadows, were Flora's playground, but her mother was wary of the road despite its quietness and, if Flora strayed onto the highway in pursuit of a butterfly, Emma called, 'Flora keep to the grinsard don't go on the road.'[1] The child stored the word grinsard in her retentive memory, where she also held a picture of the wide grass verge and its wild flowers, eyebright and harebell, lady's glove and succory. When she was grown-up she realized that her mother had been using the dialect word for greensward, an English word older than the roadside verges themselves. This little country girl who remembered these things was to write her

11

memories down when she was old, in a book which she called
Lark Rise,[2] her imaginary name for the hamlet where she was
born.

The real name of the place where Flora Jane Timms was born
on 5 December 1876 was Juniper Hill, a tiny hamlet close to the
village of Cottisford in north-east Oxfordshire. Her mother
Emma Timms was born a few miles south of Juniper Hill on the
same turnpike road to Oxford, in a small cottage adjoining the
churchyard in the village of Ardley.

Emma's parents were John and Hannah Dibber. John Dibber
was a local man from the nearby village of Stoke Lyne. Emma's
mother came from Hornton beyond Banbury. Hannah, who had
been the belle of her village, was a vain rather spoiled woman; she
was never close to her youngest daughter who was born when
Hannah was in her forties, but Emma was to be her father's
favourite child. Emma's maiden name has variously appeared in
print as 'Lapper' or 'Dipper' but it was as Emma Dibber that she
was christened in Ardley church on 19 November 1853.

Ardley church had a small gallery built in 1834 to accommodate
the handful of village musicians who provided the church music,
just as the choir of Mellstock did in Thomas Hardy's book *Under
The Greenwood Tree*. John Dibber was one of the Ardley
musicians. Like Reuben Dewy of Mellstock, he played the violin
and was also host to the other musicians who came once a week to
his cottage by the church to practise. On Sundays the singers and
musicians stood together in the gallery of the church to
accompany the congregation's hymn singing and sometimes to
perform the anthems they had painstakingly rehearsed in John
Dibber's cottage. Thomas Hardy was to realize the importance of
village church musicians and record their decline and
replacement by the ubiquitous organ. His Mellstock musicians
were Dorset men but to read about them in *Under The Greenwood
Tree*, is to know the Ardley choirmen and their leader, Flora
Thompson's grandfather.

John Dibber had always loved to make music, as a young man
he had played his violin at wedding feasts and fairs. Then when he
settled down to life as a family man, he used his beloved violin to
make music in his parish church. He was part of the old stable
rural society which began to disintegrate in his lifetime, the
society Thomas Hardy and Flora Thompson were to record in
their books.

John Dibber was a deeply religious man and music was an important part of his worship. In later years he had to sell his violin when his wife was ill and money was short. His family then thought no more of the sale of his old fiddle than selling a spare sack of potatoes in an emergency, but his granddaughter had enough imagination to realize what it must have cost him. Although Flora was not at all musical, she knew that to a musician his instrument was his most precious possession.

The Rector of Ardley, John Lowe, had his elderly sister living with him. Miss Lowe, noticed that John's youngest daughter Emma had a pretty singing voice, so she asked John and Hannah if she could teach Emma to sing. The days were long for ladies in country rectories with only sewing for the poor and reading to occupy them. Father and daughter then both practised music in their churchyard cottage.

Emma went to the rectory every day after school, there she was not only taught to sing but also to copy Miss Lowe's lovely eighteenth-century handwriting and her graceful old-fashioned manners. Emma could not fail to see the contrast between the dignified and cultured way of life at the rectory and her own home in the crowded cottage by the church. The experience taught her standards which she was to pass on to her daughter Flora.

When Emma was growing up her father was converted to Methodism and began to spend his Sundays walking the Oxfordshire lanes to meeting-houses, where he was welcomed as a lay preacher. He preached in meeting-houses which were simply the cottage homes of Methodist families who took their everyday furniture out of their room on Sundays and brought in wooden benches for the congregation and a table for the preacher. The only music at these meetings was the unaccompanied singing of Sankey and Moody hymns.

The standards of the visiting preachers varied greatly, John Dibber was considered an inspired preacher. He was also a hardworking and thrifty man who saved up enough money eventually to buy himself a pony and cart. With his own transport, he was able to give up working as an agricultural labourer and become an eggler, buying eggs from farms and cottages and selling them to shops and markets in the town.

Emma, like most girls of her class, went into service but her parents were anxious that their youngest daughter should not work in a farmhouse or a tradesman's house where the work might be rough and hard and her employers uncultured. Emma's childhood training in the Rector's house at Ardley proved useful when her parents were looking for a place for her to work. Close to Ardley was the hamlet of Fewcott where the curate Henry Jocelyne and his wife Mary needed a girl to help in their expanding nursery. Emma was intelligent, well mannered and used to rectory life, she was the ideal nursemaid for the curate's children.

Storytelling was one of Emma's many talents, a talent her own children were to enjoy and Flora to inherit. There were six children in the nursery, the eldest Louisa was close enough in age to Emma to become her friend. She was to remain Emma's friend for fifty years, sending books and toys to Emma's own children each Christmas.

Flora's paternal grandfather Thomas Timms had followed a long family tradition by becoming a mason in Bicester. He eloped with Martha Wallington, a girl from a good farming family. When Martha and the young mason eloped, they were married by special licence at Ambrosden in Oxfordshire. Although her family did not approve of her marriage, Martha still got the thousand pounds which she was left by a relative,[3] with it she and Thomas bought an inn in Oxford but the business failed. By the time Flora's father Albert was born in 1854 Thomas Timms had returned to his old trade in Buckingham, where the Timms family lived in the part of the town called Prebend End.

Flora was taken to see her grandmother in Buckingham every year until her grandmother died when Flora was eleven. Martha Wallington was a woman of some refinement who owned old china and pictures of richly dressed women. Flora remembered that her grandmother included one of Buckingham's doctors amongst her many friends. There is some doubt about the story of Martha Wallington's elopement and her inheritance, many such stories were told by poor families who lived in hope of finding lost fortunes and the Timms' family fortunes were very low by the time Flora heard the story. Albert Timms did inherit some fine miniature pictures when his mother died, however, and his sister, who had nursed Martha in her last illness, inherited china and furniture which are not likely to have come from Thomas Timms' family.

Flora's father always believed in his mother's good birth, he made sure that her surname stayed in the family by calling his third son, Flora's younger brother, Frank Wallington Timms. His belief in the fall in the Timms family fortune was to sour Albert Timms' life.

Albert Timms followed his father and became a mason, he quickly became very skilled at his craft, skilled enough as a young man to be employed on the restoration of Bath Abbey when the lathe and plaster ceiling of the nave was replaced by beautiful stone fan tracery. The experience he gained in Bath made Albert ambitious, he wanted to be a stone carver, not just a simple mason, so he went to work on other church restoration jobs, and on one of these he met his future wife.

By the time Emma Dibber met Albert Timms, she was skilled in household management and an attractive young woman. When Albert came to work on a local church, he was a fiery dark-haired young man, with strong political views. He was also an agnostic which did not recommend him to Emma's parents despite his good trade. But Emma was attracted to him and her qualifications as a wife were obvious to Albert, as it turned out he got the best of the bargain.

To begin with Albert and Emma Timms were happy enough when they set up home after their wedding on 29 July 1875. They rented a cottage at Juniper Hill, three miles from Brackley, where Albert got a job with a local builder when the work he was doing on church restoration was finished. He was to work for the same firm for thirty years repairing and extending country houses, building walls and cottages. His stone carving skill was occasionally put to use when he carved a tombstone, but most of his working life was spent on mundane building work which filled him with a brooding resentment making him a difficult husband and father.

Emma had an older sister, Harriet, living in Juniper Hill. Albert Timms had been a witness at her marriage to Thomas Sharman two years before he married Emma, and it was in her sister's house 'for convenience' that Emma gave birth to her first child Flora Jane, on 5 December 1876. The cottage, called Watford Tunnel Cottage, was later demolished. Despite Flora's description of the day of her birth as one of deep snow, records show it to have been a typical early December day of gusty showers.

Emma and Albert Timms rented two different cottages in Juniper Hill before they settled in what was called the end house, a cottage which turned its back on its neighbours and faced a big corn field known as Lark Rise, because of the many sky larks which nested there each year. The little girl who grew up at the end house would one day ensure that the field name would not be lost as so many were to be.

Albert built a small workshop on the side of the house, a temporary lean-to like the lodges which masons had set up throughout the ages. In it he attempted stone sculptures of a child's head, animals or plants but he soon gave up, allowing his personal resentments to sour his pleasure in his skills. For years unfinished carvings lay in the garden of the end house, proof of Albert Timms' unfulfilled creative urge.

When Flora was only two her mother took her to Ardley to see her grandparents. Whilst she was at home, Emma went to see the aged Rector whose sister had taught her so much. Flora dimly remembered that he gave her a china mug which had belonged to his sister as a child. The eighteenth-century mug of beautiful white translucent china, had a design of green foliage on it. Flora was always to attribute her lifelong love of the colours green and white in conjunction with her pleasure in the gift of the old mug. For years the old mug graced the mantelshelf at the end house.

For the first years of the 1880s life in the end house was fairly comfortable. Albert was paid more than the labourers who were their neighbours, so Emma was able to keep house well. Life was easiest when there were only two children in the cottage. Flora and her brother Edwin, born in 1879. Another brother was born two years later and christened Albert, but he did not survive. The next child May was not born until Flora was eight.

It is a tribute to Emma's tact and character that she was able to remain on good terms with her neighbours when she was better off than them. Her husband's sisters had married well in Buckingham and good cast-off clothes came to the end house, where Emma altered them with her skilful needle. Flora had lace on her drawers, which she tried to hide from her poorly dressed friends. They teased her so much that she took her hated drawers off and hid them in a haystack. In later years the expanding family and Albert's habit of spending his wages on drink, was to make the end house family as poor as the others in Juniper Hill.

Flora grew up in a community where almost the entire male

population and a few of the women too worked in the fields. In the census of 1881 the only men in Juniper Hill not working as farm labourers were two young men living at the inn, a shepherd, a gardener and Flora's father the stone mason. When Albert Timms' neighbours started their early morning walk across the fields to the farm, he set out alone to walk in the opposite direction to Brackley. He was already a solitary man by nature, with an uncertain temper which did not endear him to the other men of the hamlet.

Albert and Emma Timms were ambitious for their two eldest children, they wanted to move away from Juniper Hill so that Flora and Edwin could go to a better school than the small church school a mile away in Cottisford, but the move never happened. Albert began to teach Flora to read himself when the move seemed imminent; but he was sent away on a building job and Flora had to make the leap from understanding words of one syllable to real reading on her own. Once she had achieved that, she was rarely seen without a book and reading was to remain one of the greatest pleasures of her life.

She was developing other secret joys too, weather, the seasons and the wildlife of the countryside. All country children in the 1880s had to make their own entertainments but few were as aware as Flora was of the beauty around them. She was a keen observer and possessed the gifts of imagination and perception which enabled her to put her observations to use in later life. As a child her unusual gifts were simply thought odd.

From the first, Flora adored her younger brother Edwin, they became constant playmates. When the hamlet children played mud pies watering them from their own intimate water supply, Flora and Edwin were more often out in the fields looking for wild flowers or birds. They were not snobbish children but they were different. Flora had qualities and talents which singled her out early on. She was insatiably curious and could read before she went to school, qualities which made her unpopular with her friends and their parents. Flora grew into a leggy girl with dark eyes and pale-yellow hair, a combination thought most unattractive by the hamlet mothers. The hamlet children were hardy ordinary children, solid and red-cheeked. Flora's unpopularity and the knowledge that she was not considered pretty contributed to a lack of confidence which was to last all her life.

When the school attendance officer caught up with Flora she

was sent off with the other hamlet children to walk down the
long road from Juniper Hill to Cottisford school past huge fields
of ploughed earth, wheat or stubble, depending on the season.

The school in Cottisford had only one large room in which all
ages were taught. Up to forty-five children worked together,
from five-year-olds to big boys in hobnailed boots, resentful of
the time spent at school and difficult to control. It is not
surprising that the schoolmistress had little time to assess the
ability of one new pupil. So Flora was consigned to the babies'
class to chant the alphabet although she could already read.

Cottisford's schoolmistress in 1881 was Susannah Holmyard
who was to marry the squire's gardener Henry Tebby when
Flora was still in the infants' class. Sixty years later Miss
Holmyard was to appear in *Lark Rise*[4] as Miss Holmes, the
schoolmistress who married a gardener and became Mrs Tenby.
Thus lightly was her old pupil to disguise the local people she
put into her books.

Miss Holmyard taught Flora to write and by the time she was
seven Flora was writing letters to Santa Claus in rhyme to be
attached to her own and Edwin's Christmas stockings. Reading
lessons at Cottisford consisted of the class reading aloud from
selections of poetry and prose. Flora's great love of poetry dates
from her school experience of literature. Of the three 'R's
taught to her at school, the first two were to become the
mainstay of Flora's life, the third was eventually to help her to
get a job. At first she struggled with arithmetic and was bottom
of the class but she persevered and became sufficiently
competent in time to earn her living as a Post Office clerk.

Needlework had an important place on the school curriculum
in the 1880s; schools prided themselves on the work their girls
produced, but Flora was not good with a needle. Samplers
which might have appealed to her imagination, had gone out of
fashion and she was set to do a dull hemming strip. The
crumpled, bloodstained object she produced convinced her
teacher that Flora Timms was a dunce.

At home Flora began to write a family magazine[5], for which
she and Edwin composed poems and stories on grocers' grey
sugar paper until the wrapping paper changed to a dark blue on
which no ink would show. It was her first experience of a paper
shortage. Flora was destined to live through two World Wars
and very real paper shortages, but once she had started writing

she never stopped. Unknown to her teacher, Flora was reading voraciously, any book she could get her hands on, the Bible, *Pilgrim's Progress*, old books from Fewcott Rectory, even an old travel book she saw propping open a cottage window, was borrowed and read through. As a schoolgirl Flora had an inner world she was to keep to herself for a lifetime.

Flora's only real achievement at school was the winning of the Diocesan prize. Knowledge of the scriptures was thoroughly taught at Cottisford school by the Rector Charles Harrison. The children had to memorize long passages of the King James' Bible, a habit which was to lay the foundations for Flora's clear prose style. Once every year the Diocesan Inspector came to examine the children's knowledge, a visit less dreaded than the school inspector's visit. Flora was twice commended for the prize in 1886 and 1887 and she finally won the prize in 1888 with an essay on the life of Moses. Her name can still be seen in the Diocesan Inspector's report for 7 June 1888. Isobel Blaby and Sarah Cripps were highly recommended with her, so that year as so often the girls outshone the boys. Flora treasured the gilt-edged, calf-bound prayer book she won.

Outside school hours Flora had to help her mother in the house, a role which always fell to the eldest girl. As more babies were born to Emma and Albert the cottage grew crowded and Emma had her hands full. After Flora, Edwin, Albert and May, Emma had Ethel, Frank and Annie. There were to be two more babies born at the end house, Ellen and Cecil, but both died in infancy.

In old age, when John Dibber could no longer walk the Oxfordshire lanes to preach in meeting-houses, he returned to parish church worship, which was also his only source of music in a rural community. He and his wife had by then moved to Juniper Hill to be near their married daughter. Flora loved their tangled garden where she had a green study under a damson tree. Flora and Edwin played in the old pony's stable, lying in his manger and climbing in the rafters above his stall. When the pony died, John Dibber could not find the money to replace him, so he and Hannah retired to live on their tiny savings. Emma told all her troubles to her father when he came to see her every day with gifts from his garden, a little basket of early raspberries or green peas, or a tight bunch of Sweet Williams and moss roses. If anything in the house was broken he would take it indoors and mend it, or sometimes he would sit down, take a stocking out of his pocket and knit whilst he talked in a kind and gentle way to his daughter. He gave her sensible advice and she relied heavily on his wisdom and support.

Albert was drinking increasingly heavily, he was a spendthrift, sometimes bringing his wages home to Emma, often not. John Dibber dearly loved his youngest daughter and grieved for her unhappiness but he never encouraged her to be disloyal to her difficult husband. Emma helped to nurse her father in his final illness when he became bedridden and so locked with rheumatism that he had to be washed and turned over in bed. His patience and gentleness even under suffering, made a deep impression on his small granddaughter; he died when Flora was only ten. In later years she regretted that she had been too young to really appreciate the integrity and wisdom of her grandfather. John Dibber's death robbed Emma of her greatest support. Albert was an unpredictable partner and she increasingly bore the burden of raising their large family.

Flora was a sensitive and observant girl and she was aware of the struggles of the hamlet women including her own mother. She noticed women when other rural-writers-to-be were watching blacksmiths and wheelwrights, farm workers and country craftsmen at work. In the many books which were to be written about country life in the nineteenth century, women appeared only when they were part of the work force. They gained a mention as dairymaids, or house servants but the housewives who fed, clothed and cared for the village families were invisible to most observers, but not to Flora. The only other writer who has shown an awareness of women's domestic role at this time, is George Sturt who wrote as George Bourne, in his book *Change in the Village*.

The quiet stonemason's daughter helping her mother with the chores, observed everything which went on around her and she saw things from a feminine point of view. Flora soon realized that the hamlet families depended as much on the women's ability to make do, as they depended on the men's wages. When she ran in and out of neighbour's cottages on errands she saw that the hamlet women were skilled workers. They knew how to feed large families on a very limited income, they sewed, mended and made clothes, kept their houses clean without running water and worked as family launderess and nurse, all whilst coping with repeated pregnancies and the health problems which often followed. The women were frequently harassed but kind and motherly when time allowed. They would have been amazed had they known that young Flora Timms would one day record their struggles in her books, but not until she had raised a family herself and come to understand fully what their struggles must have cost them.

2 Growing Up

Like most country children Flora learned the facts of life from observation; she was a Victorian only by the date of her birth, like most country people she was no prude. As an adult she had no qualms about quoting in her books one of the maxims scrawled on the walls of Lark Rise privies[1] – 'eat well, work well, sleep well and —— well once a day.'

In matters of birth and death the hamlet children were realists. At the age of twelve Flora saw a bull in the act of justifying its existence, something she accepted as completely natural. Although the hamlet mothers went to great lengths to conceal their pregnancies, the older girls knew exactly what was happening when they were sent to the rectory to borrow 'the box' after their mothers gave birth. The box contained a baby's complete layette handmade by the Rector's daughter Grace Harrison, loaned out to supplement household supplies. Emma Timms had her own supply of beautifully made baby clothes at first, but they were wearing out by the time money was becoming scarce in the Timms family and she too had to send her eldest daughter for the box.

When one of her earlier confinements was due she sent Flora and Edwin to stay with their aunt and uncle in Buckingham. The children had to make the eight-mile journey alone and on

22

foot. Flora had taken a great liking to her aunt Ann and most of all to Ann's husband Rechab Holland, who was to become Uncle Tom in the Candleford books.

When Flora's books became well known there was some speculation as to whether Candleford was Banbury, Buckingham or Bicester. In a letter to her publisher, Flora herself said that Candleford was mostly Buckingham with something of Banbury in the picture. The home that she described there with great affection was the household of her shoemaker-uncle Rechab Holland in the market square in Buckingham.

Rechab Holland was the son of a wealthy shoe manufacturer Henry Holland. Rechab had been apprenticed to his father as a clicker and closer, a foreman shoemaker who cut out the leather for boots and shoes and then stitched the uppers. He was a widower when he married Ann Timms and by the time Flora knew him her uncle was running his own business making boots and shoes in the workshop behind his market-place home. His wife Ann was an intelligent woman, she had remained at school until she was fifteen, which was unusual for a girl in mid-Victorian times and she was in her thirties when she married the widowed shoemaker. Flora records only her aunt's great kindness, not her intelligence which Ann would have to some extent concealed: intelligence in women being regarded as a defect not an asset.

Flora's girl cousins teased her about her love of books, but on holiday in Buckingham she was allowed to read as much as she liked. At home she was often in trouble if she was discovered with a book when there were chores to be done and in a tiny cottage full of children there were always chores to be done. Flora was expected to help her mother and poor hard-pressed Emma simply could not understand her daughter's hunger for words; but Rechab Holland could. If the portrait of him as Uncle Tom is as close to the truth as all of Flora's other portraits, the time spent with her uncle was an education for Flora.

It has been said that Flora's intelligence and love of books alienated her from her roots but her background was not as uncultured as her cottage upbringing might suggest. Her parents were not rustics despite their poverty and in her uncle, Flora met a thinking man. This master craftsman was a man of intelligence, as a good craftsman has to be; he was well-read and could hold his own in conversations on literature, history and science with his social superiors. His workshop was a meeting place for all who loved to debate matters of religion and philosophy. Flora sat in the corner listening intently to these adult discussions. The views and attitudes she heard expressed supplied much that was missing in her formal education.

The background to Flora's growing years was more varied and stimulating than it might appear; it was also entirely her own. If her formal education was basic, so was that of many others who became writers and artists. Beatrix Potter, although better educated than Flora, claimed as an asset the fact that she never went to school and had an isolated childhood. People of creative ability who have to educate themselves do so in a highly individual way. They follow no curriculum, read no set books and the result is a fresh and original view of life. As Thoreau wrote, 'what does education often do? It makes a straight cut ditch out of a free meandering brook.'[2]

Flora's holidays in Buckingham were a welcome change from life at home but she was always happy to be back. As she grew older she began to take an interest in the hamlet's history, her education gave her little knowledge of national history, but her enquiring mind led her to question older people who were willing to talk to her and she learned a lot from them. A few were old enough to remember Cottisford Heath before it was enclosed in 1854, when the great corn fields surrounding Flora's home were created out of the wild-gorse-covered common. Flora noticed that old people insisted on calling the fields by old names. The derivation of the large field called 'The Heath' was obvious to her, but the field called 'The Racecourse' was more difficult to understand until she learned that races were once held on Cottisford Heath. A local historian J.C. Bloomfield quoted a contemporary account of the races in his *History of Cottisford, Hardwick and Tusmore* which was published in 1877.[3]

> Dear delightful, breezy furzy, naughty old Cottisford Heath, how does thy name carry us back fifty years to thy racecourse in each returning spring, replete as it was then with smug clean shaved squires, parsons, farmers, and traders from the towns of Brackley, Buckingham and Bicester, arrayed in deep white ties, kerseymeres, top boots, and blue or black coats; replete also with young farmers and farmer's sons, in bright green coats

resplendent with gilt buttons. How again our memory reverts to the spruce jocks, in jackets of various colours, the ladies in and on carriages, the grooms all important in their own eyes, the thickly packed pedestrians, the refreshment booths, the grandstand, the extemporised stables whose walls were faggots of gorse, and their roofs the open sky, the gambling tents, the thimble riggers, the cards with names weights and colours of the riders, and other publications vended by bawlers.

Flora would have enjoyed reading that if she could have seen it. Mr Bloomfield was writing his book about Cottisford when Flora was still at school there, if the gentleman ever saw her amongst a crowd of village schoolchildren he could never have imagined that she would write books which would outlive his and make Cottisford and Juniper Hill known to millions.

At the beginning of the century before the heath was enclosed, there were only two cottages north east of the racecourse where the juniper bushes grew. These cottages were built by the parish of Cottisford for the poor and were the foundation of the community of Juniper Hill. A neighbour who called at the end house once told Emma 'My ole granfer used to say that all the land between here and the church were left by will to the poor of the parish in the old times; all common land of turf and fuzz 'twas then but 'twere all stole away and cut up into fields.'[4] The injustices and sufferings caused by the enclosures lingered long in the memories of country people and Flora caught the echoes in her books.

Other homes had been built close to the paupers' cottages by squatters who used the common for their subsistence farming. In the 1880s Flora could still pick out the original houses which had been built in a ring on the common. They were the larger cottages of the hamlet, thatched and snug standing in gardens made on land ceded to their original owners by squatters' rights. The ground between and around these cottages was built on in the 1850s, at the time of the enclosure of the heath, to house the labourers who worked in the new fields, these were meaner homes, brick boxes with grey slate roofs.

Enclosure destroyed the livelihood of the independent English peasant farmer. It was a process which had begun in the Middle Ages and continued into Flora's lifetime. The effects on the lives of country people were devastating and were recorded by many writers to whose company Flora belongs. Oliver

Goldsmith wrote of an imaginary village ruined by enclosures in his long poem *The Deserted Village*, Thomas Bewick recorded his disgust at the enclosure of the common which had adjoined his old home at Cherryburn on Tyneside, there too juniper bushes had grown with ferns and heather, foxgloves and gorse. John Clare lamented the loss of his native heath at Helpstone in Northamptonshire, and William Barnes, born on Bagber Heath in Dorset, wrote enclosure poems. Everywhere in England cottagers and small farmers lost their right to use land which was taken in to large estates. Thomas Bewick said, 'The wisdom which dictated this change is questionable, but the selfish greediness of it quite apparent.'[5]

Enclosure was a theme rarely used by women writers, who were more often from the classes which benefited from them: Mary Russell Mitford in her book *Our Village* did rejoice that she lived in an unenclosed parish and in *Belford Regis* she wrote that, 'An enclosure bill is a positive evil to the poor.' But cottage women did not write books or poems of protest. William Barnes in his poem *The 'llotments* put these words into the mouth of John, a dispossessed commoner:

I'd keep myself from parish I'll be bound.
If I could get a little bit o' ground.[6]

The cottagers of Juniper Hill were given some ground, good allotments still lie just off the path which runs around the hamlet, but they were never large enough to provide more than household vegetables; only the older houses had enough land to grow a small crop of corn as they had always done. One of the old cottages with a large garden was owned by the couple who Flora was to call Dick and Sally in her books.

There were not many elderly people in Juniper Hill in the 1880s, independence in old age was rare in a poor community. Those too old to work went to live with their grown-up children, or if there was no one to care for them they went to the workhouse, which for Juniper Hill was the Bicester Union. The independent old couple known to Flora affectionately as Dick and Sally, were Richard and Sarah Moss.

Sarah Moss was one of the few hamlet people old enough to remember when heathland had surrounded the houses. Born in 1812, Sarah was a link between the world of the dispossessed labourer and that of her own father who had commoners' rights keeping a cow, geese, poultry and pigs on the common and owning a donkey cart to carry his produce to the market. Enclosure of common land was the first step in the process which turned the independent English peasant farmer into the twentieth-century proletariat. As a small girl it had been Sally's job to mind the cow and drive the geese over the common to find fresh grass each day. The old couple were fond of Flora and when she was old enough to be thought something of a scholar, she was asked to write their letters for them. Flora became a frequent visitor to their thatched cottage, she never forgot the comfortable rooms furnished with good oak and smelling of herbs and the hops with which they brewed their homemade ale. She loved to listen to the tales of Sally's childhood and found it strange to picture the old lady she knew as a little girl running after geese, especially as both geese and common had vanished from Juniper Hill as if they had never been. When she understood all the things which she had seen and been told as a child, Flora wrote them down half a century later.

Wages for agricultural labourers in the 1880s were very low, the families Flora grew up with were surviving on ten shillings a week, a wage which had scarcely risen in fifty years. Wages in corn country depended entirely on the price of English wheat and that price was very depressed. There was a run of very wet summers at the beginning of the decade giving poor harvests, wheat was pouring into England from the American prairies and the Russian Steppes because transport within both continents and across to Europe was able to move grain faster than ever before.

Anyone who could supplement their meagre income was lucky. Someone who could was Flora's neighbour who kept bees and made lace in the cottage behind the end house. Flora was to put this neighbour and her husband into her books as Queenie and Twister Macey. In fact the next-door neighbours were called Eliza and Thomas Massey. Many of the hamlet people were known by their nicknames, Twister's was not a complimentary one. Queenie got hers because she was married on the day of Queen Victoria's coronation and her husband called her his queen. The slight disguise of their surname from Massey to Macey, is another example of how close to the truth was Flora's picture of the Juniper Hill community.

Eliza and Thomas barely hung on to their independence.

When Flora knew him, Thomas was not too old to work but was workshy, preferring to take occasional work when it suited him. Eliza was one of the last of the hamlet lacemakers. On the census return for 1881 only one girl, Elizabeth Cross, put lacemaker as her full-time occupation.

In the 1840s and fifties lacemaking had been common in that north-east corner of Oxfordshire, where women had learned to make beautiful Buckinghamshire lace from the county over the border. Before the advent of machine-made lace, pillow lace could be sold to the dealers at Banbury fair for a good price.

Eliza Massey made lace because she enjoyed the craft, though there was little money to be made from it and she often gave it away. Her next-door neighbour, Emma Timms, was discerning enough to prefer handmade lace to the coarse machine-made product and she was pleased when Eliza gave her lace to trim her babies' clothes. Emma had a natural good taste which Flora inherited. Flora saw the era of cottage crafts coming to an end. It was one of the many commonplace things which she stored in her retentive memory.

Eliza Massey also kept bees and she made a few valuable extra pence when the dealer came to buy her honey. Twister died when Flora was still a child, years later she heard that when Eliza was beyond housekeeping and managing her bees, she was taken into Bicester Union, the dreaded workhouse.

Flora and her brother Edwin remained very close throughout their childhood, sharing their love of the countryside and books as much as they were able to. Life in the end house became difficult when their father Albert grew more and more morose, returning home late in the evenings flushed with drink.

In later life Flora was to be very reticent about her relationship with her father. In some ways father and daughter were alike, both creative self-contained people. Flora was one day to say that her father had all of the bad qualities of genius and few of the good ones. When she was very small Flora had been her father's pet, her great need for love nourished but, as his view of life soured, his relationship with his sensitive daughter suffered. Albert's drinking increased to the point where his work suffered too, his unsteady fingers often failing to control his mason's tools, he became an unreliable workman slowly downgraded from mason to bricklayer.

Flora had been proud of her father's skills, never tiring of the tales of his work at Bath Abbey when he had carved stone, working from a dangling cage in places inaccessible from a ladder, 'for all the world like a giant spider dangling from that slender thread in space,'[7] her mother told her. Flora loved to picture her young father helping to create delicate fan vaulting in such a great building. His later neglect both of his work and of his family was a deep loss to her. Fortunately her uncle in Buckingham set her higher standards of masculine behaviour and her affinity with her beloved younger brother was to give balance to her view of men.

It was a hard life for their mother who had seen more civilized ways. Emma was to have ten pregnancies in all, losing four children; so, by the time Flora was in her teens, Emma had little time to spare for her eldest child who was something of a puzzle to her. Flora's talents were not those her mother understood and she was beginning to despair of finding a suitable job for her. At thirteen Flora was still at home with no idea what she wanted to do with her life. Most of the young girls from the hamlet were in service by the age of twelve but Emma wanted something better for her daughter. She had wanted Flora to follow in her footsteps and become a nursemaid in a gentleman's house but Flora was not interested in babies. She was in no way qualified for the job, she was actually nervous of handling babies, useless with a sewing needle and by her mother's standards dreamy and impractical. What could Emma do with a girl who always had her nose in a book and who scribbled stories on every available scrap of paper? There was no money to keep Flora at school where she had shown no unusual scholastic ability beyond incessant reading.

What Flora wanted no one knew, least of all herself. She and Edwin nursed romantic plans to live together in a cottage. Edwin's ambition to work on the land was one which horrified his parents who wanted him to learn a trade. How envious Flora and Edwin would have been of William and Dorothy Wordsworth if they had read of the story of their life together in the cottage at Grasmere. To share a life of long walks, poetry and gardening would have been the ideal of Flora and Edwin. But the Wordsworths started far higher up the social ladder than Flora and Edwin Timms. There were no rich friends or legacies coming to help them, they were going to have to earn their livings.

Flora always felt that her mother liked boys more than girls. It was still common for sons to be cherished more than daughters; mothers actually taught their sons to regard girls as inferior beings. No wonder Flora felt unwanted sometimes when her mother told her that she was not pretty and had no skills to offset the misfortune of being female. Emma was not being unusually cruel, life was hard for women and good looks, if you had them, were an asset. It is sad, however, that she convinced her daughter that she was unattractive. In fact Flora merely failed to conform to the current standard of beauty, she had a wide generous mouth when rosebud lips were admired and she was thin when curves were thought womanly and plumpness was a sign of prosperity.

An answer to the problem of Flora's future came in the form of a letter from an old friend of Emma's, Kesia Whitton who ran a village Post Office at Fringford a few miles from Juniper Hill. Kesia wrote to say that she needed an assistant and thought that Emma's eldest daughter might do for the job. Mrs Whitton had been born in Stoke Lyne where some of Emma's cousins lived, she was twenty years older than Emma but they had known each other for a long time.

When Albert approved and the offer was accepted, Emma began to make new clothes for Flora, and Albert was persuaded to make a trunk for her. The trunk was studded with brass-headed nails forming Flora's initials FT, initials she was never to change even when she married.

Flora viewed the prospect of her new life with mixed feelings. Leaving home and her much-loved brother was a wrench but one that she would have to make sooner or later to provide for herself. She had already met Mrs Whitton and liked both the lady and her small Post Office, and Fringford was not far away from Juniper Hill, she would be able to walk home if she had a day off.

The offer of a job as an assistant Post Office clerk was a stroke of luck for Flora. She could never have entered the Post Office in the normal way which involved taking the Civil Service examination, which was deliberately set at a higher standard than girls like Flora from elementary schools could attempt. The Post Office wanted its official female clerks to be ladies and so made the entry qualifications high, at one time even introducing a foreign language to an already academic examination. Male clerks took a different exam, the Post Office was less concerned with their social standing. Cottisford school had not prepared Flora for official entry into the Civil Service, she had the intelligence but not the education.

To work in a village sub-Post Office she needed only the ability to read and write well and to add up swiftly, all this Flora could do well by the age of fourteen. She also had a good deal of common sense inherited from her mother and a quiet charm of her own which was to enable her to get on well with the customers she was to serve. A village Post Office was to prove to be a good place for a future writer to work in. Flora was to be associated with the Post Office all her life.

When the time came for her to leave Juniper Hill, she had her trunk full of new clothes, an exercise book given to her by Edwin in which she was to keep a journal and a new half crown from her father. The pony and cart had been borrowed from the Fox Inn so that her father could drive her to Fringford.

Her going was not unnoticed, any break in routine was of interest in that small community and brought neighbours to their cottage doors. They watched Flora get up beside her father, her plaited hair looped and tied with a businesslike black bow to go with her new grey dress. Her trunk was loaded, her father was impatient to be away. Everyone wanted to say goodbye, her mother, all her small brothers and sisters and the neighbours who called out good advice and their good wishes. As the pony moved off Flora turned to catch a last glimpse of her old home and much-loved family but they were soon lost to view as the pony walked from the track onto the road and out of the hamlet.

Flora was only to return to her home again for occasional Sundays and rare holidays. She had spent only fourteen years and a few months in the hamlet but she was to cherish her memories of Juniper Hill for half a century when she would recreate it as *Lark Rise*.[8]

3   On Her Majesty's Service

Flora and her father arrived in Fringford in the middle of the afternoon. Around the green the village was quiet in the May sunshine, children were at school, men at work and the women finishing their Monday chores: the shops were deserted.

Candleford Green in Flora's book is a composite place, created by her from all the villages in which she worked but Fringford is where she began her Post Office career and Mrs Whitton, the postmistress there, was the main subject for her portrait of Dorcas Lane.[1] When Flora knew it in the 1890s, Fringford was a thriving community of over 400 people with a butcher, a shoemaker, two general shopkeepers, a plumber, a carpenter, a brick manufacturer, a publican and a baker. A carrier travelled daily between the towns of Banbury, Bicester, Brackley and Buckingham. There were two blacksmiths in the village, one of them doubled as a baker perhaps firing his ovens from his forge, the other blacksmith was Mrs Whitton's husband John.

John Whitton died shortly after Flora's arrival at the Post Office-cum-forge, so it is possible that her services as an assistant were needed to free Mrs Whitton to look after her husband. The couple's son Alexander had died two years earlier in 1889 in Africa, where he had been local auditor of the Gold

Coast Colony. Alexander must have inherited his mother's good business brain but he died at twenty-four, a victim probably of one of the many tropical diseases which killed young colonials in their thousands in the nineteenth century.

Kesia Whitton had undertaken the running of a sub-Post Office in her home to provide a much-needed service for the village and perhaps as an occupation for herself, although she did not close the forge when her husband died. Like the redoubtable Dorcas Lane in *Candleford Green*,[2] Kesia Whitton opted to run the forge herself. She had been doing the paperwork for some years before her husband's death, so she simply continued to manage the forge, employing a foreman and several young smiths to do the work. In a directory published in 1895 Mrs Whitton had the occupations, blacksmith, farrier and Post Office, entered against her name.

Flora admitted when she wrote *Candleford Green*,[3] that Dorcas Lane was a portrait with elements of more than one of the postmistresses she had worked for in her character. But some of the people at Fringford Post Office are as recognizable as Juniper Hill people, with only slight changes of name. For example, the real maid at Fringford Post Office was Zilpha Hinks who appears in Flora's book as Zillah the maid who presided over the workmen's tea table and sometimes grumbled at having a teenage girl in the house to be fed and looked after.

Photographs of Kesia Whitton show her to have been formidably stout, John and Kesia Whitton both weighed over eighteen stone. Although Flora describes Dorcas Lane in her book as being of slight build, to disguise Kesia Whitton, she could not resist describing in *Candleford Green*[4] the lavish tea provided for her arrival, a tea of new-laid eggs, scones, honey, homemade jam and fresh Banbury cakes. She was to write, 'Miss Lane ate enough for two of them. Food was her one weakness. She loaded her scone, already spread with farm butter, with blackcurrant jam and topped it with cream.'

Albert Timms did not stay to share tea with Mrs Whitton and Flora, he had relations to visit nearby in the village. So soon after her arrival Flora found herself in strange surroundings without any of her family to support her.

She was shown the Post Office after tea, although she could not start work until she had been sworn in before a JP the following day. The Post Office was much as Flora described it in her books. In the long thatched house a counter had been made over the passage which ran from the front door to the garden door. There are still screw holes in the beam inside the front door of the old Post Office where the lifting counter could be hooked up, to allow access between front and back doors. On the counter stood brass scales; there were pigeon holes for all the official forms and drawers held stamps and postal orders. Although part of the old Post Office garden has been built on, there are still three wells outside just as Flora described them in her book, including the one close to the back door, rediscovered when a flagstone gave way beneath a lady visitor who only saved herself from falling further by supporting her body on her arms until help came. The blacksmiths' working well is still under a cover in the path between the old forge and the wheelwrights' shed.

One thing was not as Flora described it on her arrival, there was no telegraph machine in Fringford at that date, the nearest telegraph office was at Stratton Audley. The telegraph machine under its velvet teacosy cover, which appears in *Candleford Green*,[5] belongs to the later part of Flora's time in Fringford.

At the Post Office Flora had a room to herself for the first time in her life, a room with pink washed walls, chintz curtains and a chest of drawers. She was tired on her first night but not too tired to sit up in her bed beneath the window looking out into the damp garden-scented darkness before sleep claimed her.

Next morning she had to walk alone to the nearby manor house for her interview with the local JP. It was a very nervous Flora who was ushered in to the JP's room by a footman and announced as 'the young person from the Post Office'. Luckily the gentleman was kind and took an interest in her home and family after the business of swearing to promise and declare that she would 'not open or delay or cause to be opened or delayed any letter or anything sent by post'.[6]

On her return to the Post Office Flora began her training, like all new employees she was to be bewildered at first by all the official forms and the minutia of the job, but it was all within her considerable capability.

Although Flora was not to immortalize Mrs Whitton and her Post Office until 1943 when she wrote *Candleford Green*,[7] she did write a much earlier story called *The Education of a Genius*,[8]

only fifteen years after she left Fringford. In this story the wife of
a village blacksmith tries to find an extra source of income so
that her clever son can stay at school. Mrs Welstead, the
blacksmith's wife, offers her services to an official who is looking
for a suitable place in her village for a Post Office. 'I've kept the
books for my husband since we were married,' she tells the
official, 'we could run a counter up across the front passage.'
The final sentence of that story reads, 'and so it was that Mrs
Welstead became the mother confessor of her parish'. Kesia
Whitton was certainly the mother confessor of Fringford.
Possibly only the vicar or the doctor know as many secrets in a
village as the postmaster or postmistress, even today. As a Post
Office assistant Flora was to be privy to many secrets.

Despite her elementary education Flora was quick to learn
and she soon grasped the complexities of Post Office work in a
way which might have surprised her old school teacher. She
responded quickly to the stimulus of a new life where every day
she learned new skills and met new people. In her room she
could read in peace, she had new status too, she was no longer
simply the eldest and overburdened daughter of a large family,
or the stonemason's girl, she was the young lady at the Post
Office and the customers liked her.

Flora was never vain, she had been told too often that she was
not much to look at, but she was sensitive enough to know when
people liked her, and her country customers soon showed their
liking in ways that she understood and enjoyed. They brought
her posies of cottage garden flowers with which she filled the
Post Office and some brought her their choice apples or pears;
like any young girl Flora enjoyed being liked and such homely
gifts made her very happy. Early photographs show Flora to have
had a gentle expression with soft brown hair which had
darkened to match her dark eyes, she was as attractive as most
young girls are. In the office she wore a black silk apron over her
grey dress with a seasonal flower pinned on her breast, a rose in
summer, snowdrops, her favourite flowers in wintertime.

Her day's work began very early in the old outhouse which
had been turned into a sorting office, where she opened the mail
bag brought in by the postman who had walked from Bicester,
the post town four miles away. In the 1890s postmen were paid a
flat rate of sixteen shillings a week for which they often walked
sixteen miles in a day carrying loads of up to thirty-five pounds,

so it is hardly surprising that the Fringford postman was inclined to grumble about the weather, which he thought 'was ordered by someone with a special grudge against postmen'.[9] The rural postman's round was not to be eased until bicycles were introduced at the turn of the century. In a few places men who owned a pony and cart sub-contracted their time to the Post Office, but for regular postmen it was 'Shanks' Pony' all the way until 1900.

The postman who had walked from Bicester had a welcome rest when he reached Fringford Post Office where he had to sort the letters for the village. Flora's job was to sort the letters for outlying houses and farms into piles which were then handed to the two women letter carriers who delivered the cross-country letters. Such unofficial rural letter carriers as these women were to disappear from the country scene and were replaced by uniformed postmen when daily free deliveries finally became universal at the end of the decade.

Flora worked a long day, from the early morning letter sorting, until the Post Office closed in the evening, at eight or even nine-thirty in the summer. She had no half-day at first and only a rare Sunday off as there was a Sunday morning delivery to sort and a Sunday evening dispatch. But Fringford's was not a busy office and there were times in each day when Flora could read behind the counter as long as Mrs Whitton did not actually see her doing so. When the Post Office was quiet, only the muffled noises from the forge and the grandfather clock in the kitchen marked time as Flora was absorbed in the worlds of Thomas Hardy, George Eliot or the Brontës. If Mrs Whitton came into the office her book was hidden under the counter. The telegraph bell often tore her from the foggy world of Dickens' London to deal with the everyday problems of an Oxfordshire village.

In summer, the garden door behind the Post Office counter was kept open and customers could see through into Mrs Whitton's garden crammed with cottage garden flowers growing in wild profusion. The open door gave Flora a view of roses and lavender, pinks and peonies. Her visits to the privy were a pleasure in summer if not in winter, as the path went through the flower garden and a bower of nut trees planted to preserve the modesty of visitors to the earth closet. Mrs Whitton encouraged Flora to walk in the garden when the Post Office was not busy, and her special joy in hot weather was a shady area of ferns, bushes and Solomon's Seal in a part of the garden which was always damp and green.

Occasionally Flora was allowed time off to travel with the carrier. Mrs Whitton suggested that she took out a library ticket, when she had read her way through all the books in Mrs Whitton's house. Bicester had a large reading room in the 1890s beneath the assembly rooms and also a free public reading room and it may be from one of these places that Flora was able to borrow books. With her library ticket Flora read her way through Dickens, Trollope and Jane Austen. At the Post Office she had already read Shakespeare, Scott and the major poets. She had developed a taste for poetry at school where she read extracts from famous poems in reading lessons, but literature had not been taught to her as a separate subject in her village school. However, it is unlikely that she could have learned more in any school for young ladies, than she learned from her own eager reading of the books she borrowed. She began to write poetry herself in the privacy of her room overlooking Fringford Green; she was to think of herself as a would-be poet for half a lifetime but it was as a writer of prose that she was eventually to succeed.

During the 1890s Mrs Whitton agreed to have a telegraph machine installed. She was shown how to use it and then she trained Flora in a skill which was to prove very useful later in her career. The Post Office at Fringford was issued with a machine already old-fashioned in the 1890s but easy-to-use and reliable. It was the ABC machine invented by Sir Charles Wheatstone in 1840. The ABC was a visual telegraph machine which indicated the letters of the alphabet so that the receiving operator wrote the message down letter by letter and sent messages in the same way. Flora learned to use it easily. Later she was to learn morse code to enable her to operate newer machines in the other Post Offices where she was to work.

Once she had learned to take down incoming messages, Flora was shown by her employer how to send a telegram, first turning a handle on the machine which operated a bell to engage the attention of the receiving clerk at the office nearest to the telegram's destination, then pressing the key 'A' for attention and 'T' for telegraph before beginning to spell out the message by pressing the keys around the alphabet dial.

Even though it was an out-of-date machine, the telegraph was a great boon to the people of Fringford giving them, for the first time, a means of rapid communication with the outside world. The telegrams which they sent and received were not all life and death messages, those who could afford to could order goods from the town or arrange transport to meet an arriving train at Bicester station. The prompt delivery of incoming telegrams was sometimes difficult, small offices like Fringford could not keep a regular delivery boy.

In *Candleford Green*[10] the telegrams were delivered on foot by a young girl from a nearby cottage. If she was already on her way to a distant farm when another telegram came in, the Post Office maid or one of the forge apprentices had to go: telegrams were never kept waiting. Telegrams were expensive to send and, until 1897, expensive to receive, after that date delivery was free up to three miles from the telegraph office.

Flora could remember when the people of Juniper Hill had had to find three shillings and sixpence, half a day's wages, to receive the news of a relative's illness or death. Even after the three mile rule was introduced, plenty of outlying farms and cottages more than three miles from Fringford had to pay for their telegrams. Flora felt the burden her poorer customers had to bear keenly when they paid dearly for the bad news she so often had to convey to them.

Although Fringford is off the main road, it is close to a long stretch of old straight Roman road so it is not remote. On Tuesdays and Fridays the carrier travelled to Bicester, on Wednesday he went to Brackley where Flora's father worked. Thursday was Banbury's market day and on Saturday he went to Buckingham, so Flora was not cut off from family and friends. She sent her washing home every week by the carrier and received in return a parcel of clean clothes. When Flora left home her mother had five small children to care for without her elder daughter's help but she still found time to enclose something in with the clean laundry to remind Flora of home. The home-baked cakes, garden flowers and tiny pots of jam she sent, show Emma to have been a kind and thoughtful mother.

The long letters which she also enclosed with the fresh-pressed clothes were even more indicative of Emma's qualities, her accounts of the news from home and the hamlet were so witty and racy that Flora wished in later years that she had kept them. If Emma's letters to her daughter had survived they would add much colour to this distant period of Flora's life.

There was a Timms family living in Fringford who may have been related to Flora's father. The head of the household was Henry Timms who had been born in Bicester and was a mason by trade who had married a Fringford woman. Male members of the Timms family had been masons in Bicester for generations, so it seems likely that Henry and Susannah Timms and their four children were related to Flora which may have helped her to feel more at home in Fringford.

Flora endeared herself to the old and poor amongst her customers whose problems she understood well. There were few pensions to be paid out over the counter, state pensions for the old were not to be given until Lloyd George's social reforms of the next decade. But there were a few old soldiers who came to collect their service pensions and they found in Flora a patient listener to their stories of India. The stories caught Flora's imagination and on the rare occasions when she walked home to Juniper Hill to spend Sunday with her family, she told Edwin the exotic stories that she had heard. Edwin was becoming restless and eager to see the world, within a few years he was to enlist in the army and see Africa and India for himself and discover if the stories told to his sister in an English Post Office, were true.

Flora grew very fond of some of her regular customers. A few of the oldest ones could remember the days before the penny post, when poor people could not always afford to accept the letters sent to them, which had then to be paid for by the recipient. The cheap postal service had been in operation for fifty years when Flora started work and was a great boon to families with daughters in service in faraway towns or other family members living away from home. Those with sons in the army serving overseas, or with relatives living in the dominions, followed the campaign for the Imperial Penny Post with interest. Flora and Mrs Whitton too followed the developments in *The Times*.

In 1890, the year before Flora had started work, the Post Office had organized a great Jubilee dinner to celebrate fifty years of the Penny Post and those who spoke then raised the recurring question of an International Penny Post. The movement had begun in the 1850s, and it continued throughout

Flora's time at Fringford. In 1898 there was a conference on
what was then called Imperial Post for the colonies, presided
over by the Duke of Norfolk, the Postmaster General. Mrs
Whitton enjoyed following the arguments for and against cheap
postage for the Empire. It gave her the feeling that she was
working for an international network, despite being tucked away
in rural Oxfordshire. She was genuinely interested in politics
and the issues of the day, her businesslike brain enjoyed current
affairs. Flora took an interest on a more personal level. Edwin
was at that time planning to emigrate to Canada as soon as he
was eighteen, although the war in South Africa was to alter his
plans, and her younger brother Frank was keen to go to
Australia, where he eventually became a fruit farmer in
Queensland. Imperial Postage was not to be introduced until the
turn of the century and even then not all the colonies took part.

So Flora and Mrs Whitton went on in the 1890s weighing
letters addressed to distant parts of the Empire. Flora knowing
better than her employer what a sacrifice sixpence or a shilling
was out of a meagre cottage budget. Half a century later she was
to capture on paper the joys and sorrows of life in an English
village in the 1890s.

4   Youthful Joys

During her time in Fringford Flora endeared herself to the Post Office household. At fourteen she had been a pale lanky girl but Mrs Whitton's good food had turned her into a lively teenager: her figure rounded and her cheeks pink. She was so full of energy that even Zilpha, the grumpy old servant found her useful as she ran upstairs to save Zilpha's old feet, or out into the garden to fetch the washing in before a shower. The younger blacksmiths called her 'Missy' and showed her new kittens in the woodshed or choice blooms in the garden. Matthew the elderly foreman teased her kindly. After her rigorous childhood, Flora found life in a houseful of older people very pleasant. At the Post Office she soon occupied a position not unlike the indulged daughters of local shopkeepers who became her friends.

Fringford was a much livelier place than Juniper Hill had been for a young girl to live. There were church socials and penny readings to attend and Fringford Green was a focal point for outdoor social gatherings like the hunt meet and Fringford feast day. For such events Flora had a grandstand view from the Post Office. She was by nature an onlooker, not one of the crowd, her unusual powers of observation made it a pleasure for her to watch on such occasions, to absorb their atmosphere and commit them to memory. She was never to forget the sights and sounds of the huntsmen with their horses and dogs thronging the green on January mornings. The fair held on the green made a vivid impression on her too as she leaned out of her window after work in the evening, to watch the crowds around the shooting gallery and the coconut shy.

Although Flora was a quiet girl she did take part in some of the modest pleasures available to country girls in the nineties. She learned to ride a bicycle when the new safety cycles were all the rage and it was possible to hire a machine for sixpence. Flora's wages did not go far but she sometimes spent sixpence to enjoy the freedom of the lanes. A few young women shocked onlookers, by appearing in knickerbockers but Flora could not have afforded such a garment if she had had the courage to wear it. When she went cycling, she managed by tucking her long skirt modestly around her legs, only she knew that her petticoats had been left behind on her bed in the pink-washed bedroom under the Post Office thatch.

Church socials were not much to Flora's taste although she was sometimes persuaded to go with the tradesmen's daughters, dressed in her confirmation dress of nuns' veiling. They played party games after tea, supervised by the curate and his Sunday school teachers, it was unsophisticated entertainment but Flora was not a party lover. At one of the socials she met a young reporter with whom she corresponded for a time afterwards. In both *Candleford Green*[1] and *Heatherley*[2] a young reporter appears briefly. It is tempting to speculate how Flora's life might have turned out if she had married a journalist.

The village girls who became Flora's friends were not cottage girls, many of them lived over or beside shops run by their parents. Their lives were easier than Flora's, most had their own rooms and pretty clothes, and only light domestic duties were expected of them. Flora knew that she was not really one of them, her background was too humble and her clothes unfashionable. But, although she was not popular amongst the set, she was a good listener and their light-hearted company saved her from being too serious.

Annual outings were a feature of village life which Flora often heard about from her customers over the counter. The school children went in a waggonette to have tea and play games in a neighbouring village, the mother's meeting went to London Zoo and the church choir went to the seaside, Bournemouth or Weston-super-Mare. Listening to the excited accounts of these trips retold in the Post Office, Flora cannot have dreamed that she was to spend thirteen years of her life in suburban Bournemouth.

Of all the entertainments available in Fringford Flora liked the penny readings best. The National School built in 1886 was an ideal meeting hall. The schoolroom was only a short walk along the village street but for Flora, full of anticipation, the walk had the spice of excitement as she carried a lantern out into the dark, for an evening of dramatic renderings of Dickens, Thackeray or Scott. It cost one penny to get in but Flora reckoned it a fine pennyworth. The readers were local people and the pieces chosen either by the readers themselves or by popular request. Fifty years later Flora commented that despite their obvious enjoyment the audience rarely borrowed the books from the parish library to read for themselves. She did not criticize their failure to read, she astutely recognized that they had been a public waiting for radio and the cinema.

Amongst the young people who became Flora's friends in the village was the grandson of the village carpenter John Rogers who made the organ case for the parish church. Young Willie shared Flora's taste for books and poetry, pleasures she had only shared before with her brother Edwin. On summer evenings after the Post Office closed, the two young people sat at the bottom of the garden under the nut trees reading Keats and Shelley, Flora was happier and more carefree than she had ever been before.

Mrs Whitton did very little entertaining at the Post Office but every summer she gave one party which Flora was to recreate in *Candleford Green*[3] as the hay home supper. The supper was a country custom already dying out but Mrs Whitton liked to keep such old customs alive. After the hay was cut in the two small paddocks which she owned, her friends and employees sat down to a roast pork dinner to celebrate the cutting and carrying of another hay harvest. Although the house which Flora knew has only garden ground behind it now, old maps show a long narrow field behind the old Post Office and another beside it, even today local people remember that the fields once belonged to the Post Office. If Flora had been born even a decade later it is doubtful if she would have been one of such an old-fashioned gathering. The provisions never varied from year to year.

Indoors, the kitchen table was laid with pies, tarts and custards and, in the place of honour at the head of the table, the dish of the evening, a stuffed collar chine of bacon. When the company assembled, large foaming jugs of beer would be drawn for the men and for those of the women who preferred it. A jug of homemade lemonade with a sprig of borage floating at the top circulated the upper end of the table.

The customers who used Fringford Post Office came from all levels of society and inevitably Mrs Whitton and Flora got to know many of their secrets in the course of business but bound by their sworn oath they kept it all to themselves. Letters bearing crests and coronets passed through the Post Office, telegrams were received from, and sent to, public figures known to the gentry in the area. Family secrets and love affairs were known at the Post Office and Fringford was fortunate in having a discreet girl behind the counter, a gossip would have caused havoc.

But Flora was not universally popular. Inevitably with such a comfortable job she was sometimes on the receiving end of someone's jealousy, which once took the form of an anonymous letter which worried her for weeks. She used the device of anonymous letters in one of her books to show what trouble they can cause in a small community.

In an encounter with an upper-class customer in the Post Office Flora displayed her ability to voice her own opinions at a time when the young were expected to bow to the opinions of their elders. A local lady invited her to join the Conservative Primrose League, an offer which Flora declined politely telling the lady 'We are Liberals at home.' It was a brave stand for a young girl in her position and she recognized it as a milestone in her own mental development. Flora was to remain a Liberal all her life, although she admired some socialist efforts on behalf of the poor.

At the bottom of the social ladder in the village were the Irish farmworkers who arrived each summer to take the harvest. Other country writers have written about the annual arrival of Irish farm labourers. Alison Uttley wrote of the men who came to her father's Derbyshire farm – 'brown-skinned, blue eyed, swarthy, with their trousers tied below their knees with twisted bands of grasses, with a wild rose in their battered hats and a clover stalk between their teeth'.[4]

The Irishmen on her father's farm came to cut hay, Flora's Irishmen came to cut corn. They sent the money they earned home to their families in Ireland and it was for just such transmissions of small sums of money that postal orders had been introduced in 1881, replacing money orders. But postal orders could not be sold on Sundays or after office hours on Saturday, when the men had been paid and had time to visit the Post Office. So Mrs Whitton, who was kind, as well as businesslike, sold postal orders to the farm-hands illegally and let Flora do so too. Flora performed another service for the shy and often illiterate men who came into the office out of hours, she wrote their letters for them. As the men told her what they wanted her to write down she noticed, 'there were none of the long pauses usual when she was writing a letter for one of her own old countrymen, as she sometimes did. Words came freely to the Irishman, and there were rich, warm phrases in his letters that sounded like poetry.'

Flora wrote letters for gipsies sometimes too including Cinderella Doe, who was 'tall for a gipsy, with flashing black eyes and black hair without a fleck of grey in it, although her cheeks were deeply wrinkled and leathery. Someone had given her a man's brightly coloured paisley-patterned dressing gown, which she wore as an outdoor garment with a soft billy-cock hat.'[5] This splendid woman told Flora's fortune in return for her letter writing, predicting that Flora would be loved by people she had never seen and never would see. A pleasing, if puzzling, fortune for a young girl working in a village Post Office.

Flora would have been surprised if she had been able to look into the future to a time when her name would be coupled with that of Anthony Trollope in books of Post Office history, as two famous literary Post Office employees. Such a link with one of her heroes, and such achievement for herself, was beyond her wildest imagination.

Of all the Post Office jobs which Flora had to do, the one she enjoyed most came her way by accident. One winter's morning one of the women letter carriers had to leave work on receiving bad news; she went so suddenly that she left her pile of mail half sorted on the outhouse sorting-office bench. Mrs Whitton needed to find a replacement quickly to take the letters to the outlying farms and cottages and more important still, to take the bag of mail out to Shelswell Park, the mansion home of Edward Slater Harrison Esq. Flora who had long been missing her old freedom of the fields, tentatively volunteered to go. To her surprise and delight her offer was immediately accepted.

Flora set off with the mail bags that morning, well wrapped against the cold. There was frozen snow on the ground but she had two hours of freedom and she loved every minute of it. As she was eventually to write in *Candleford Green*[6]

> She never forgot that morning's walk. Fifty years later she could recall it in detail. Snow had fallen a few days earlier, then had frozen, and on the hard crust yet more snow had fallen and lay like soft, feathery down, fleecing the surface of the level open spaces of the park and softening the outlines of the hillocks and fences. Against it the dark branches and twigs of the trees stood out, lacelike. The sky was as low and grey and soft-looking as a feather bed.

The letter carrier never returned to work and her job was offered to Flora for an extra four shillings a week. Her parents gave their consent grudgingly. Albert and Emma Timms thought it a very odd job for a young girl to do, but they agreed and Rechab Holland was given an order for a pair of stout waterproof shoes for Flora to wear with her ordinary clothes. Uniformed post-women were not to become a common sight until the First World War.

And so began a time filled with delights for the sixteen-year-old post-girl. She did find a few difficulties in her new role, the footmen at the big house teased and harassed her, cows barred her way and she met a strange young gamekeeper who wanted to make her his girl, but none of these things could spoil her real pleasure, being out in the fields again. Even at sixteen Flora had the gift of appreciating small beauties unconsidered by most passers-by. The commonplace was never common to her, she had the artist's seeing eye. Even on dull days, when her long walk across the fields was wet and muddy, she always enjoyed herself.

The landscape through which she passed was not spectacular, it was, and is still, a pleasant undistinguished piece of English countryside but Flora loved it. When other girls of her age trimmed fashionable hats with ribbons and bought new shoes for the spring, Flora delighted in wreathing wild flowers around her old straw hat, still wearing her stout shoes powdered with pollen. She gloried in wild flowers, carrying great bunches of them back to the village to fill pots and vases for her bedroom and the Post Office kitchen. 'The copses were full of bluebells, there were kingcups and forget-me-nots by the margins of the brooks and cowslips and pale purple milkmaids in the meadows.'[7]

In years to come Flora was to be a well-informed amateur botanist and ornithologist in Hampshire but her interest in all country things had its roots in Oxfordshire.

During this time Flora was sometimes able to walk home to spend a Sunday with her family. Her brother would walk part of the way to meet her and her two small sisters waited on the road. As they neared the house on one of her visits, she saw her father examining the broken branch of damson tree with one eye on the road to watch for her. She was greeted with a kiss as warm as she could have wished for. Perhaps once she had moved away, Albert missed her and realized her worth. They were so alike that father and daughter could have been devoted, but Albert's problems and his unreliable affections made Flora cultivate that detachment which is invaluable to a writer. Like Jane Austen who she so much admired, Flora was becoming emotionally independent. Nevertheless she enjoyed her day at home and found that she was on a different footing with her mother who treated her like an adult and shared her amusement when Flora discovered that she had grown so tall that she had to lean down to take her mother's arm.

In *Candleford Green* Flora was to describe a one-sided romance which occurred during her letter-carrying days. A young gamekeeper began to accompany her on her post round and paid her much attention. He was a rather cold calculating young man who decided that she was his girl with very little reference to her feelings. He caught her at the kissing gate on her round sometimes and wanted her to meet his parents but he was so self satisfied that he did not notice that Flora, failed to return his feelings. If the events Flora recounted did take place they were in character. Although Flora was attracted to the life of a gamekeeper's wife in a cottage on the green, she was too sensible to tie herself at sixteen to a cold young man. She was wary of men and marriage having observed her mother's trials.

Flora could have spent a lifetime in Fringford; Mrs Whitton said she would like her to take her place when she retired, although in fact Mrs Whitton was to die in 1898, not long after Flora left Fringford. But it was not Flora's destiny to be a village postmistress. Although she might have had a happier life if she had remained close to home, literature would have been poorer if exile from her home county had not eventually resulted in the writing of her Oxfordshire books at the end of her life.

After Queen Victoria's diamond jubilee in 1897 Flora began to want to see more of the world. So she gave in her notice having applied for the first of a series of jobs which were to take her out of Oxfordshire for the first time in her life. Mrs Whitton was not pleased at her going, nor were her parents. But Flora was by then no longer a shy young girl, she was over twenty years old and restless. Mrs Whitton had kept a strict eye on her since she was fourteen, she was more than ready for a measure of independence.

On the day of her last post round she made her last visit to the pond where the yellow brandyball waterlilies grew, the boathouse where she had sheltered from a thunderstorm and the hill from which she once saw a perfect rainbow. As she was later to write: 'She was never to see any of these again, but she was to carry a mental picture of them, to be recalled at will, through the changing scenes of a lifetime.'[8] Flora left Oxfordshire never to return except for short holidays, but she took with her a store of memories which she would one day share with countless lovers of the English scene.

5   Further Afield

Flora left Fringford to see more of the world and also to gain experience in larger Post Offices. She knew that she could not pass the Civil Service examination to gain entry to the official Post Office establishment. As an unqualified assistant she needed to gain as much practical experience as she could to further her career. Her parents did not see it that way. As Flora was to write years later, 'They looked upon experience as something to be gathered unconsciously, not a thing to be sought. They preferred permanence and security.'[1] No doubt they would have preferred Flora to have remained under the eye of Mrs Whitton and close to home, they were alarmed when she applied for distant jobs and travelled to them alone.

Flora was one of an army of young women at that date who were no longer satisfied with the old order. As a book on housekeeping explained to employers of servants at the turn of the century, 'The young working girl of today prefers to become a Board School mistress, a Post Office clerk, a typewriter, a shop girl, or a worker in a factory, anything rather than domestic service.'[2]

Flora had not been in domestic service with Mrs Whitton but she had been living in with a friend of her mothers who kept as strict an eye on her as any employer of servants might have done.

Her first job outside Oxfordshire was probably at Twyford in Buckinghamshire, the next in Essex; she left Fringford after the Diamond Jubilee in 1897 and in later years she was to say that she saw her first moving film at Halstead in Essex in 1898. Had Flora been able to join the Post Office establishment as an official clerk, records of her employment might still exist to tell us exactly where she worked during those years. Her future husband's employment records from 1891 to 1935 still exist in the national Post Office Archive, but the sub-postmasters or mistresses Flora worked for chose their own unqualified assistants whose names never appeared on official pay rolls.

In *Heatherley*,[3] a book not published in her lifetime, she wrote that after leaving her home county she had seen, ' ... an Essex salt marsh, blueish mauve with sea lavender and a tidal river with red fisher sails on it and gulls wheeling overhead and seaweed clinging to the steps of its quays'.

How long Flora spent in Essex is uncertain but she had more than one job, for she later referred to returning to the Post Offices in which she worked then, to do holiday relief jobs.

In one of her posts Flora learned to use the single-needle telegraph machine which, unlike the ABC machine she had used in Fringford, used morse code. Once she had become proficient in the use of morse and could operate two different types of telegraph machine, Flora was then well qualified for a job where she would be in charge of a sub office. That opportunity arose when she saw an advertisement for the job of clerk in charge of the sub-Post Office at Grayshott in Hampshire. Flora had never seen Hampshire and she enjoyed exploring areas new to her. The Grayshott job also offered some responsibility for which she was ready.

The postmaster at Grayshott, Walter Chapman was a furniture maker of some talent, the Post Office was a sideline which brought in a regular income for his family between commissions for furniture. His woodwork took almost all of his time, so he had very little to do with the Post Office beyond employing staff, organizing their work and being responsible for the money. Mr Chapman had had to advertise for a new counter clerk when the lady he employed left suddenly on the verge of a nervous breakdown. She was a well-qualified woman having previously worked in the Central Telegraph Office in London, but the quiet life which this nervous lady had sought in

Grayshott had proved far from peaceful as Flora was to discover for herself.

Flora was able to offer more than six years' counter experience and proficiency with the single-needle telegraph machine in use in Grayshott, she got the job. Full of happy anticipation Flora travelled to Grayshott by train, her journey taking her through London where she had time to go shopping between train connections. She left her luggage at the station to go in search of a new hat.

Flora had only one pound to see her through to her first salary at the end of the month. She spent almost half her savings on her new hat, a very feminine way to boost her morale: she was always to show a lively interest in fashion. The hat cost nine shillings and eleven pence three farthings and was made of beaver and matched her travelling costume of a brown dress and waist-length cape. The hat was probably the popular toque shape. Hats in the late nineties were often lavishly trimmed with flowers, ribbons and plumes. The hat which Flora chose was decorated with only two ostrich tips, she was very happy with it, feeling that it went well with her brown hair and dark eyes. The bright fashion colours of the eighties had given way to quieter colours, navy, grey and brown were popular, so Flora was quite in fashion in her brown outfit. The dress had been made for her with skirt length just clear of the ground for country wear. As it turned out it was just as well she was not wearing sweeping skirts, for she was to have an unexpected long walk at the end of her journey.

The second part of her train journey took her from London to Haslemere, on the Surrey–Hampshire border, a journey of an hour and a half. It was a fine warm afternoon when Flora left the train and stood outside Haslemere station expecting to see her employer who had promised to meet her train. But when all the passengers from the London train had dispersed, Flora was left alone. Eventually she decided to walk to Grayshott. She left her luggage in the booking office to be sent for later and set out on foot.

As Flora walked out of Haslemere and began her four-mile walk, she saw the commons and downs which surround Grayshott, including Bramshott and Ludshott commons which she was soon to know well.

The commons on that September afternoon were covered

with heather in bloom and Flora was captivated. Her preconceived ideas of heather country, culled from her reading of Sir Walter Scott, paled before the glories of the Hampshire hills. Without knowing it, she crossed the county boundary and passed from Surrey into Hampshire where she was to spend much of the next thirty years of her life. Had she known that when she first walked into Hampshire she would have been happy with the knowledge, for she fell instantly in love with the landscape of birch trees, bracken, heather and pine. After her train journey the air exhilarated her with its refreshing resinous smell and the views delighted her to such a degree that she was sure she had made the right decision in taking her new job. When she walked into Grayshott itself she found the village equally pleasing, its two roads lined with tile-hung shops and houses under steep red-tiled roofs. The Post Office stood gable-end on to the road, also a red-tiled building under wide wooden eaves. Sadly it was demolished in 1986 so we can no longer see the shop which Flora entered at the end of her long walk.

Flora's high hopes for her new life were somewhat dampened by the strange atmosphere which she sensed as soon as she entered the living quarters behind the Post Office. Emily Chapman, the postmaster's wife, was there to welcome her. She was a sad-faced woman of thirty-seven in late pregnancy who apologized when she realized that her husband had not met Flora as arranged and she had walked from the station alone. Flora was shown her bedroom and later she took over her duties in the Post Office and met the girl who was to be her junior, eighteen-year-old Sarah Symonds who was to be a cheerful companion for Flora in that gloomy household. Flora soon realized that there was more to the atmosphere of the Post Office than the effect created by its dark, heavy furnishings and lack of light. There was something fundamentally amiss in the household. The outgoing assistant warned Flora that the postmaster and his wife had dreadful quarrels, domestic staff rarely staying long because of them. She dismissed the problem as normal domestic strife between an incompatible couple. Flora was perceptive enough to realize quickly that the problem went deeper, however, and time was to prove her tragically right.

She met her employer on her first evening; a disconcerting man, who crept up behind her laughing silently. Walter

Chapman at forty-four was a good craftsman and a good businessman, but his manner showed signs of the mental instability which was so soon to surface. Flora was not at all sure how to take him, his manner towards her was pleasant, but his wife and children were clearly afraid of him.

When she started work the next morning Flora quickly made friends with Sarah Symonds. She had a pleasant, cheerful nature and shared Flora's love of books and poetry. The two girls spent twelve hours a day together so it was fortunate that they enjoyed each other's company. Outside working hours they saw little of each other, Sarah had a fiancé and her own family and friends.

There were other young people employed by the Chapmans, a succession of young girls came to work in the house and left, frightened away by the domestic strife. Mr Chapman had a young apprentice in his furniture workshop, Gilbert Winchester. Flora and Sarah as business girls saw little of the other employees, but they too were acutely aware of Mr Chapman's rages and his wife's fear of him. In the tragedy which was to take place within two years, both Sarah, Gilbert and the current servant were to be called to witness to the angry scenes they had so often overheard. Flora, the only employee who lived in, could have told even more, but she had left before matters came to a head.

One of Flora's first jobs at the Post Office was to train Sarah to use the telegraph machine. This was kept on a shelf under the stairs, between the Post Office and the back living room. Whilst using the machine in this position Flora and Sarah could not help but overhear the domestic disputes which went on so often and so loudly a few feet from where they were working. Flora hated the atmosphere and was soon very tempted to look for another job but she had no money and no wish to add to her mother's burdens by calling on her help. Emma Timms had no spare money with young children still at home and very little money coming into the house. Albert was drinking too much to be of help to anyone and Edwin was far away, fighting in South Africa, having enlisted just as he was about to emigrate to Canada. Flora travelled by train to Aldershot one snowy evening to see her brother off when he enlisted. Brother and sister had an hour together on the cold platform, he full of excitement, she full of fears for his safety.

Edwin was to be taken prisoner by the Boers and abandoned in the Veldt where he almost died of thirst. His life was saved by a gift of water from a Boer woman at a farm he stumbled into after three days of walking. Luckily for Flora's peace of mind she was not to hear that story until Edwin was safely back with his regiment. Letters and information about her brother in South Africa were rare.

The news from South Africa, in that winter of 1899 was very bad, English troops were besieged at Ladysmith, Mafeking and Kimberley. It was one of Flora's jobs to post the latest news of the war in the shop window of the Post Office when she had taken down the message from the telegraph and each time she had to write out bad news, her heart ached with fear for her brother.

Flora's greatest consolation in this unhappy time was the countryside around Grayshott which she began to explore in her precious free time. Her first months in Grayshott were the months of late autumn and winter, she worked from eight in the morning until eight in the evening, by which time it was too dark to walk. On Sunday she had to man the telegraph machine for two hours until the war news came through, not until ten o'clock was she free to make her getaway. Flora was a great walker, she had had to walk long distances like most Victorian children, from an early age, the daily walk to Cottisford school, the long walk which she and Edwin made when they were sent to Buckingham and her time as a letter carrier, had all taught her the joys of being afoot in the countryside in all weathers. So she was more than happy to spend her Sundays alone walking the Hampshire hills and valleys.

She explored the valley which runs south from Grayshott, in which there is a series of small lakes known as Waggoners Wells. This beauty spot was to be given to the National Trust in 1919 but in 1899 when Flora was discovering the valley, the area was just a local beauty spot, deserted on Sunday mornings. The lakes are in deep woodlands of sweet chestnut, oak, birch and pine, the edges of the lakes are overhung with beeches. In wet weather the valley bottoms are very wet but when she could get to them Flora loved these marshy places with their moss gardens.

Marsh pools held a fascination for her, she would stand for hours on a quaking island of rushes to observe pond life like an absorbed child. She described one of these occasions in *Heatherley*:

Newts with smooth dark backs and orange undersides would glide out silently from beneath her feet; frogs squatted sedately, like fat elderly gentlemen, under umbrellas of fern fronds; butterflies hovered in the warm air over the pools, and dragonflies, newly emerged from their chrysalids, dried their wings and darted away, miracles of blue and silver. In the clearer pools, Laura's own birth plant, Sagittarius, floated its arrow-shaped leaves, and there were other water plants, water flowers, and water leaves and mosses in abundance. Once she found a few spikes of the bog asphodel, its constellations of yellow starlike blooms shining against the dark rushes, and once, on the heath above, one solitary spike of the rare field gentian, of a heavenly blue.[4]

Better even than the pretty valley Flora loved the open heath. Here her long walks took her up to the freedom of Bramshott or Ludshott commons where she walked the sandy paths across gorse- and heather-covered land. It was on these commons that she met a few country people who retained commoners' rights, a lifestyle she had heard about in her childhood at Juniper Hill. The smallholders survived largely by supplying their butter, eggs and garden produce to the new residents and holidaymakers who were coming in increasing numbers to what were being called the Surrey Highlands. Flora also met the broom squires, who earned their living from making garden brooms or besoms from the abundant heather which was cut, tied in bundles and stored for use in thatched ricks beside the broom squires' cottages. The brooms were made by tying bundles of the stiff dry heather together with strips of hazel, ash or oak and given a handle of ash or lime wood. The smallholders and broom squires were some of the last independent cottagers Flora was to meet and she never forgot them, especially Bob, who lived with his sister on a tiny smallholding. Bob had three fields and kept a few cows which he milked in the outbuildings beside the tiny cottage hidden in a valley. Flora was captivated by his store of heath lore, Bob knew every flower, bird, beast and reptile on the heath and he could take Flora to see any nest or rare wild flower she wished to see. She asked him to show her an adder as she had never seen one and Bob took her along a sandy heath path one day, to a spot where they waited until an adder glided across the path. People in Grayshott thought Flora's friendship with such a simple man odd, even improper, but Flora had enough discernment even at that age to value his knowledge and wisdom.

Flora was not the only lover of country life and crafts in the Grayshott area at that time. A movement called 'The New Crusade' had its headquarters in nearby Haslemere where they worked for, 'the restoration of country life, in place of the modern manufacturing town, and of country crafts instead of mechanical industries'. A crusade doomed to failure by the birth of the twentieth-century. Flora mentioned their *Simple Life Press* in a short story and probably visited the church where they practised simple Christian worship. Thoreau and Tolstoy, were two of their prophets whose work was known to Flora.

Rambling over the commons Flora continued her self education as a naturalist, using her copy of Gilbert White's *Natural History of Selborne* and her own marked powers of observation as guides. Out of doors around Grayshott Flora was entirely happy, indoors she was unhappy. The situation in the Chapman household was deteriorating and Flora began to hear strange noises in the night. Mr Chapman had taken to prowling around the house in the dark, even opening Flora's bedroom door. She put up with her uneasy fears until one night they turned to terror when Walter Chapman fired a revolver at imaginary burglars. When Flora rushed out on to the landing in her nightdress she found her employer holding a revolver and his wife trying to coax him back to bed. He spoke wildly of enemies with whom he thought Flora was in league. After her night of terror, Flora began to look for new lodgings.

Finding lodgings was not easy, people with rooms to let in Grayshott could make more money accommodating visitors, than housing young working girls on low wages like Flora. Briefly she boarded with retired Londoners who wanted company for their daughter but the lack of privacy soon had her looking elsewhere. She finally settled in the front upstairs room of a working-class household. The room was too poorly furnished to be let to summer visitors but it was clean. Flora had grown up in a home with few luxuries so she was entirely happy with her new lodgings. Quiet and solitude were luxuries to her. She had a bed, a table where she could write, bookshelves and an easy chair by the fire, for which she paid four shillings out of her pound a week wages and got a skimpy high tea provided as well. Flora was truly independent at last. After her childhood in the crowded cottage, life under Mrs Whitton's sharp eye and the sinister atmosphere of Grayshott Post Office, a room of her own was a joy. She still worked long hours and had to eat her midday meal on duty so that she could listen for the telegraph machine, but her evenings became pure pleasure.

On fine light evenings Flora walked in the woods or on the heath, if it was wet she could curl up at her own fireside with a book. She wrote very little at this time having arrived at what she called 'the age of disillusion'. From her earliest childhood she had been in her own words, 'a great despoiler of paper', writing stories and verses with Edwin, keeping her journal after leaving home and writing more verse in Fringford. But at Grayshott she met some of the successful writers who lived in the area and for a time she felt her own small talent to be unworthy of development. For the rest of her life Flora was to feel guilty whenever her pen was idle but for this short time she was too awed and impressed by the talent around her to have confidence.

She found herself serving at the Post Office, writers like Conan Doyle, Grant Allen, Bernard Shaw and Richard le Gallienne. The Surrey Highlands had been discovered as a healthy place in which to live and a number of writers and artists made their homes there. Conan Doyle had a large house called Undershaw near Hindhead where he hoped that the downland air would cure his consumptive wife. He was already a very well known and popular writer. Flora was still young enough to be very impressed by well-known people and she enjoyed seeing the famous come into the Post Office where she sometimes could not help overhearing conversations when such people met in the small shop. Her weighing of letters, or search for official forms, was sometimes accompanied by literary conversations between famous customers. She was quite well-read enough to have joined in, but courtesy prevented her from doing so and propriety did not permit Post Office employees to converse with customers. Besides which Flora was always a listener not a talker. She enjoyed going to local lectures on spiritualism, vegetarianism, the Boer War and the Balkans, several times she heard Bernard Shaw speaking on socialism.

Serious matters did not absorb all Flora's free time, however, nor was she such an intense young woman that she did not have time for friends of her own age and of both sexes. Flora in her early twenties was an attractive and intelligent girl with a sense of humour and ironic wit which soon brought her friends. She got to know the young shop assistants in the village and the daughters of small shopkeepers. This group of girls spent their free time together having picnics and tea parties, playing games and sharing popular jokes. Flora had much less free time than most of them but she was sometimes able to join in the picnics and parties. The girls had one common ambition, to get married and set up home and to this end they all spent endless hours embroidering items for their bottom drawer. This was a pastime Flora did not share, she hated sewing and her natural good taste did not admire the current fashion for decorating every possible item of household linen with flowers embroidered in crudely coloured art silks. Flora had no use for embroidered hair tidies and egg cosies and she sometimes silently compared the proud owners of bottom drawers to 'hen birds hoarding straws, before a mate appeared or the site of a nest was decided upon'.[5]

Flora did not tell her friends about her long walks, they would have thought her very odd, even fast, a young woman did not roam about the countryside alone then, without someone suspecting that she was going to meet a lover. Flora kept her love of literature to herself too. Although her friends frequently quoted from popular books of the day, a true bluestocking was regarded with horror, they believed that an intellectual girl would never find a husband. There were at that time dozens of magazines aimed at girls and young women, *Girls Own Paper* was very popular, as was *Home Chat* which survived until 1958. *The Lady*, to which Flora would one day contribute essays, had already begun its long career. Whilst her friends were swopping women's magazines for the stories and embroidery patterns in them, Flora was buying back numbers of the *Quarterly Review* to read in the privacy of her rented room.

Flora made other friends during her time at Grayshott, if her account of that time written in *Heatherley* is as close to the truth as her other books to which it was the sequel. But these friendships cannot, at the time of writing be verified. Until the census returns for 1901 are open for study it is not possible to trace all of Flora's Grayshott friends. The first of these, who Flora called Mr Foreshaw, was a retired African game hunter who wore white tropical suits in summer and in winter protected himself from the English cold in a long coat worn with a sealskin cap with ear flaps tied under his chin. He employed an ex-serviceman to keep house for him and was thought to be a woman hater but Flora won his friendship by stamping letters for him, because his arthritic fingers could not easily manage stamps, she also delivered a telegram to his bungalow after the Post Office had closed one evening. To thank her for that service, Mr Foreshaw invited Flora to tea, it was to be the first of many hours she spent in his bungalow, though it was a friendship which she kept secret from her younger friends who would have thought it an odd, even improper friendship.

Mr Foreshaw had courteous old-fashioned manners and treated Flora with a consideration that delighted her. Despite his reputation as a crusty bachelor, he remembered her femininity and on her first visit to tea, Flora was shown into a room where she could tidy her hair, a room which he had prepared for her with eau de Cologne and a paper of pins.

She found his African stories fascinating and admired the trophies which filled his home. Mr Foreshaw was a lonely old gentleman who shared Flora's passion for books, though he preferred Victorian writers, Dickens and Thackeray to the contemporary writers Flora was reading at that time. Their friendship lasted for a year until Mr Foreshaw died suddenly. He had wanted to leave his books and trophies, his maps and his butterfly collection to Flora, because he felt that she would care for them but he died without making legal arrangements. The entire contents of the bungalow were auctioned and Flora was saddened to watch from the Post Office window as people passed carrying her friend's household goods which they had bought. Flora tried to buy her old friend's favourite book *Vanity Fair*, from a woman who came into the Post Office carrying a bundle of books marked with a lot number but the woman would not part with one. Some of the African objects went to a museum though no one but Flora knew the stories attached to them, she was left with only her memories of Mr Foreshaw but these have proved more enduring than the artifacts since he is now immortalized in her book *Heatherley*.[6]

Mr Foreshaw was an enigmatic man whose background Flora never knew but she liked him for 'his originality, raciness, his immense store of experience and his biting wit'. Raciness was a quality Flora mentions often, her mother's letters to her she said were often racy, clearly she admired vigour and directness in

letters and conversation and was spirited enough herself to enjoy
a little spice in others. In one of her later stories Flora included
an elderly man whose talk was 'as spicy as ginger'. That was
written perhaps with fond memories of Mr Foreshaw who kept
rare dainties in his store cupboard, guava jelly and dry ginger,
and rare stories in his memory which Flora never forgot sharing.
She was exceptionally fond of aged people, whose memories she
enjoyed hearing and whose characters she admired. Mr
Foreshaw seems to have enjoyed her company as much as she
enjoyed his, young as she was then, Flora too was an original.

The other friends who appear in *Heatherley*[7] are Richard and
Mavis Brownlow, a brother and sister who stayed with relations
near Grayshott. Who these friends really were we may never
know, but it is significant that Flora wrote of the time spent in
their company, as the high-watermark of her youth. Richard and
Mavis's lives at home were not happy, their father had died
suddenly and their mother suffered such a severe depression
after his death that the atmosphere in the London house was
permanently gloomy, made worse by the loss of a comfortable
income. On holiday in Hampshire Richard and Mavis were
freed from burdens which were heavy on their young shoulders
at home. Richard was clearly attracted to Flora, the three young
people shared a love of literature and the countryside which
Flora was able to show them. In return Richard and Mavis took
Flora to stay at their home in London.

Flora was never to forget the London which Richard and
Mavis showed her, a city of crowded gas-lit streets, smelling of
orange peel, horse manure and wet clothes. They took her on
Sunday to Threadneedle Street where she gazed on the outside
of the Central Telegraph Office where she considered working
and where she may indeed have worked as a telegraphist a few
years after this visit. She later was to write in *Heatherley*:

> Now she saw Fleet Street and Johnson's Court, passing without
> the faintest anticipatory thrill the office of the magazine whose
> editor would one day accept her first shyly offered contribution
> ... That walk through the silent, deserted City was one of the
> richest memories of Laura's later years. She would not have
> missed seeing it as it was then; nor would she have willingly
> missed seeing the very different Saturday night scene in the
> shopping quarter, or the suburban home of her friends; and still
> less would she have cared to miss the sensation of freedom and

homecoming she felt when, at the end of her train journey, she came to the heath and once more breathed the odours of heather and pine and saw the starry heaven above the pine tops.[8]

Whilst Flora enjoyed the friendship she was unaware that Richard viewed her as more than a friend; she was taken aback when later he declared that they could never marry because of his family problems. Marriage was a distant prospect to Flora, an inevitable future but one she was in no hurry to seek, she was enjoying her freedom.

Richard and Mavis encouraged Flora to think of working in London and for a time Flora followed a correspondence course which was to lead to the Civil Service examination and a London job. She had problems with arithmetic and geography, her schooling in Cottisford was inadequate for the course, but her essays gained good marks. One piece on the subject of Henry James' *Portrait of a Lady*, provoked a handwritten comment from her tutor as well as the customary mark. He wrote, 'Don't care for James's work myself but almost thou persuadest me.' Clearly Flora could analyse literature and write a good essay even in her early twenties. But she knew her limitations, or at least the limitations of her education, and she gave up what she later called, her one bid for worldly advancement. Had she passed this examination Flora would have become a member of the official Post Office establishment and her subsequent movements would have been easier to trace. Richard and Mavis Brownlow were very disappointed when she gave up her course and she was never invited to their home again. They were hurt by her decision, especially Richard who still nourished romantic ideas about their friendship which embarrassed Flora. Her friendship with the young Londoners faded.

6 A Murder and a Mystery

The new century began officially on New Year's Day 1901, on the 22nd of that month Queen Victoria died and everyone went into mourning clothes. Rich women ordered new black dresses, those too poor to keep a funeral outfit in their wardrobe, dyed their old clothes or sewed on crepe bands. Flora could not afford new black clothes, so she made do with her dark serge skirts which she wore with stiff-collared blouses and a dark tie, an old coat dyed black did service for three months until grey was allowable and she could wear the grey tailormade coat and skirt which was her best outfit. Flora was always interested in clothes and she loved colour. In the winter of mourning she loved to see

> ... the gipsies of whom there were many living on the heaths, wearing bright colours. They were indeed more colourful than usual in their dress, for they reaped a rich harvest of cast-offs of the sudden unfashionable red, blue, and green shades which the original possessors decided it was no good keeping, as the styles would be hopelessly out of date before their new black was discarded. For the first three months after the death of the queen only the attire of the gipsies provided a splash of colour in the gloom; then, as the days lengthened and brightened, black and white mixtures and soft tones of mauve and grey began to

appear. Finally, women's dress that year went purple. Wine, plum, pansy, heather, and lavender shades were in great demand.[1]

All her life Flora was to have a romantic affection for the gipsies. She once tried to learn the Romany language from a gipsy girl with whom she had made friends. In the end she learned very little but she taught the young gipsy girl to read. One of Flora's earliest short stories to appear in print, was to have a gipsy heroine.[2]

At twenty-four Flora was ready for another move, she had no close friends to keep her in Grayshott and the atmosphere at the Post Office was becoming intolerable as Walter Chapman's behaviour deteriorated. Although Flora no longer lived at the Post Office she had never forgotten her night of terror when her employer had fired his revolver at imaginary intruders. She wrote: 'Even in moments of personal happiness, she was aware, if but dimly, of a sinister cloud in the background.'[3]

Then a new telegraph office opened not far away and Grayshott Post Office suddenly lost much of its trade. With telegrams sent and received down by eighty per cent Flora became redundant. She made arrangements to leave early in the spring and where she went first we do not know, but before the mystery of Flora's whereabouts in 1901 and 1902, there was a murder.

Shortly after Flora left Grayshott Emily Chapman left the Post Office too. She took her four young children and fled after her husband again threatened to shoot her. She was not a local woman and had few friends, she was also heavily pregnant with her fifth child. Hers was a desperate position. By all the standards of the day she was in the wrong as a runaway wife, but to his credit Mr Chapman's brother Ernest, a successful builder in the area, gave his sister-in-law a temporary home in his house in the village.

Ernest Chapman knew that his brother was under the delusion that his wife was unfaithful to him and that he often threatened her life. Sadly Walter Chapman managed to stage a reconciliation and persuaded his wife to return home for the birth of their child. Within weeks of her confinement he was again accusing her of infidelity, his pathological jealousy becoming obvious to all who knew the family. One day in May he sent a telegram to the postmaster of Petersfield which read, 'Diabolical plot to ruin me,' but still no one took any action to help him, and Mrs Chapman and her four children were left unprotected at the Post Office. In June Emily Chapman gave birth to her fifth child. She was by then utterly terrified of her husband. She spoke to the doctor who attended her confinement. However, he considered Walter Chapman to be deluded but not certifiable.

On the morning of 29 July 1901 the Chapman's servant, a girl called Annie Harding was upstairs looking for clothes for the six-week-old baby who was to be bathed. She heard the other children begin to scream and ran downstairs to the living room where she saw the baby on the floor and Mrs Chapman covered in blood in Mr Chapman's arms. The terrified young servant picked up the baby and ran outside for help. In the workshop, the apprentice Gilbert Winchester also heard screams and ran down the village street to fetch Ernest Chapman. The two girls in the Post Office, Sarah Symonds and Flora's replacement Edith Smith, also ran into the street. Grayshott had become a place of terror on a fine quiet summer morning.

Ernest Chapman arrived and ran into the house to find his sister-in-law dying on the living room floor, she had twelve stab wounds in her chest and wounds on her arms and legs. Emily Chapman had fought hard for her life. Later when a doctor examined her body, a cabinetmaker's carving tool was found embedded four inches into her back.

Flora read the reports of the murder in the newspapers and was deeply disturbed. For weeks she tormented herself with the thought that if she had told someone what she knew of her employer's behaviour when she had lived at the Post Office, she might have prevented Mrs Chapman's death. In the newspaper report, she read Ernest Chapman's evidence that his brother had threatened his wife with a revolver months before the murder. Flora realized that only she knew that Mr Chapman had actually fired his revolver during the night on at least one occasion when she slept at the Post Office. She knew that she should have reported her employer's behaviour to the police but she knew also that she might have had a very unsympathetic hearing, the police did not like to interfere in domestic strife at that time, though the use of a firearm might have made them respond.

Flora would almost certainly have lost her job by reporting the incident but she would have felt less guilty when the murder happened. Having said nothing she felt that she bore some portion of the blame for Mrs Chapman's death, blame borne by everyone who kept silent knowing her to have been in danger. Emily Chapman was as much a victim of the current attitudes to marriage, as she was a victim of her husband's madness.

The case was fully reported in the *Hampshire Chronicle* and from its pages Flora saw that the two Post Office girls had had to give evidence to the Coroner's inquest held at The Fox and Pelican inn, Grayshott two days after the murder and a week later they were called before the magistrates' bench at Alton. Only the servant Annie Harding and Gilbert Winchester gave evidence when the case reached the Hampshire Assizes in Winchester in November, as they had both seen Mrs Chapman dying; the two Post Office girls saw nothing, having run out into the street for help. Flora knew that she had missed a horrific and prolonged experience. Walter Chapman was found guilty but insane by the jury in Winchester and was sent to Broadmoor. Flora had by then taken a job in what she called 'a distant part of the county'. In time the murder became for her 'one of the sadder pages of memory' and one which she recorded in *Heatherley*.[4]

There is now a gap in our knowledge of Flora's life. What we do know is that she left Grayshott early in 1901 and at sometime during the next two years she met the man she was to marry in 1903.

John Thompson was born in Ryde on the Isle of Wight on 4 April 1874; he was one of the large family of Henry and Emily Thompson. Henry Thompson had been a Chief Petty Officer in the Royal Navy but by the time John met Flora, his father was a naval pensioner. John's mother Emily Thompson was a formidable lady who was very strict with her ten children, as no doubt she needed to be with so large a family to bring up on a naval pension in a small terraced house. It has been said that the Thompsons looked down on Flora because she was born in a cottage. If they did consider themselves more respectable it is likely to have been by virtue of Henry Thompson's naval past. Albert Timms had become a mere bricklayer according to the birth records of the last child Emma bore him in 1900.

Emily Thompson had been determined that all her sons and

daughters should be trained for secure jobs and so Jack, as John Thompson was always known to his family, left home at the age of seventeen to work on the mainland in the Post Office. He started work in April 1891 training to be a sorting clerk and telegraphist in Bournemouth. He was to remain in the Post Office service for forty-four years. As John was starting his training as a Post Office clerk and telegraphist in Bournemouth, Flora was doing the same job on a smaller scale, in the little Post Office in Fringford.

It seems likely that John and Flora met in Bournemouth, which may be the distant part of the county to which Flora went in 1901, at that time Bournemouth was in Hampshire. Margaret Lane in her biographical essay on Flora[5] states that the couple met when John was a Post Office clerk in Aldershot, but John Thompson did not work in Aldershot. His employment records, which still exist, show that he was continuously employed in Bournemouth from 1891 until 1916 when he became postmaster of Liphook and had been married to Flora for thirteen years.

If Flora met John in Bournemouth in 1901, she did not marry him then, because the next record we have of Flora is at an address in Twickenham in January 1903. Searches have not revealed what took Flora to London. Possibly she left Bournemouth to fulfil her ambition of Grayshott days to work in London, and found herself a job in a sub-Post Office in Twickenham. With its literary associations, Twickenham had much to attract Flora. Curiously the road in which she found lodgings, Heathfield Road North, is close to an area called Whitton; did fond memories of Mrs Whitton and Fringford take her there? In her later writings Flora mentioned Kew which she visited at this time. For a country girl like her even leafy Twickenham seemed like a busy town. When she tired of pavements and houses the green open spaces of Kew offered escape. The formal areas held little appeal for her but she loved to walk in the woodlands and by the lakes.

Flora married John Thompson on 7 January 1903 at the parish church of St Mary The Virgin, Twickenham. Whether John and Flora had kept in touch when she moved to London and intended to marry, or whether he pursued her to Twickenham is not known.

John's family were represented at the wedding. One of the witnesses was his brother George Thompson who worked at the

Central Telegraph Office in London. It is possible that Flora went to London to work at the Central Telegraph Office and met John through his brother. She was a trained telegraphist and the Central Telegraph Office is mentioned more than once in her books. The building which Flora knew dated from 1874 and was being extended at the turn of the century to meet the rapidly developing telegraph service. In December 1940 The Central Telegraph Office was gutted by fire after a wartime raid. Many records were destroyed so we may never know if Flora worked there but the fact that George Thompson did is attested by his family and his name appears as a witness on John and Flora's marriage certificate.

It seems that there were no members of Flora's family at her wedding. Emma still had children at home, Albert had his job and there was little money to spare for train journeys to London and even less for accommodation or wedding clothes. Flora's beloved brother was in India. Although the Boer War was over when Flora married, Edwin's regiment had been sent straight from Africa to India. He served for five years in India and his infrequent letters must have reminded Flora of the tales of life in India which she first heard as a young girl at the Post Office in Fringford. Edwin had his photograph taken in uniform, and Flora treasured the picture of her brother looking very military and mature. If he had been on home leave when his sister married, Edwin could have given her away looking very fine in his uniform, but there was no home leave for soldiers in India. In the absence of her father or her brother there is no record of who gave Flora away.

St Mary's Twickenham is a riverside church with a medieval tower and a Georgian red-brick nave. Flora was no doubt pleased to be married in a church where so famous a poet as Alexander Pope is buried, though she might have preferred to be married in her own home church in Cottisford. When she came down from the chancel of St Mary's Twickenham a married woman, she passed the stone incised with the letter 'P' which marks Pope's grave. Did thoughts of her own literary ambitions enter Flora's mind as she left Twickenham church, or was she entirely preoccupied with the knowledge that as Mrs John Thompson she had taken on domestic responsibilities which would keep her busy for the rest of her life? Whatever her thoughts and the realities of her married life, Flora was to see her name in print within seven years of her wedding day.

7 Wife and Mother

Flora and John Thompson made their home in Winton, a township on the outskirts of Bournemouth. Their first rented home, No.4 Sedgley Road was a typical small suburban house at the very edge of Winton's development. Edwardian Bournemouth was expanding fast and areas like Winton were being encouraged to provide - housing and transport for Bournemouth's workers, to prevent overcrowding in the town centre. Beyond Sedgley Road other roads were merely marks on the map and pegs in the ground when Flora and John set up home.

John Thompson worked long hours as a sorting clerk and telegraphist at the main Post Office in Bournemouth; once he left home in the morning Flora was on her own. She had had to give up her job on marriage, the Post Office did not employ married women. But she had plenty to occupy her, housework was time-consuming in Edwardian homes, the young Thompsons were too poor to have any help in the house and Flora had learned high standards of housekeeping from her mother so she spent much time cleaning, cooking and washing. Shopping took time too, before her marriage she had lived happily on apples, bread and milk, now she had to feed a husband and make a slender housekeeping budget stretch.

When she went shopping in Winton, Flora was surrounded by more building and development. Rows of shops were being built along Winton's main road, there were still some old shops but everywhere that Flora walked with her shopping basket, she saw new shops being built, some of them in grand parades styled on developments in the centre of Bournemouth. Winton was a busy and growing suburb in 1903 with traffic and trams on its main road.

If she had time to spare in the afternoon Flora could escape from suburbia by walking towards Talbot Village, only a ten-minute walk from her house. To get there she had to pass through the remnant of countryside in which new roads were being laid out, where she and John were eventually to live. It was her favourite type of countryside of pine and heather, but the pine trees were being pulled down by great steam-driven traction-engines and the ground cover of bracken and heather grubbed up to make way for the builders. Flora did not care to linger near this scene of destruction, but a short walk further west took her over the county boundary into Dorset where Talbot Village was (and still is) a Victorian island hidden from the encroachment of Bournemouth by woods and gardens. Twenty years later Flora was to write fondly of her rambles amongst the Dorset pine woods. There she could be out of sight and sound of the developers, to enjoy the woodland walks and the atmosphere of an estate village. It was an atmosphere in which she felt entirely at home.

Talbot Village was a model village laid out forty years earlier by two wealthy Victorian sisters. Over 400 acres of common land had been enclosed but unlike Cottisford Heath, a large area, 150 acres of Talbot land had been left as heath for common use. The village had been created with a church, a school and nineteen Gothic cottages each with an acre of garden. It was a thriving community when Flora knew it, with almost 100 children in the small school. In some ways the village reminded her of Juniper Hill, despite the more picturesque cottages and their larger gardens, but the cottagers of Talbot Village were much less free than those of Juniper Hill had been. There were rules to which they had to conform, the head of each household was responsible for the proper behaviour of females, in independent Juniper Hill the cottages were not tied nor their occupants bound by rules. The rent of the tied cottages of

Talbot Village was half a crown a week where Juniper Hill cottagers paid only a shilling a week or at the most two. But Flora enjoyed the contrast between the rows of shoulder-to-shoulder suburban houses in which she was living and the pretty village so nearby. She could admire their gardens, buy garden produce and even admire the pigs which they were allowed to keep, it was a solace to an exile. The remaining heath too was a substitute of sorts for the wild heathlands of Hampshire which she had loved so much.

Another of Flora's favourite walks was to a house called Skerryvore which had belonged to Robert Louis Stevenson in 1884 and which he named after the lighthouse built by his family in Argyll. Flora loved the creeper-covered white brick house for its associations with Stevenson whose work she admired. In it he had written *Kidnapped, Dr Jekyll and Mr Hyde, A Child's Garden of Verses* and many other minor works until his tuberculosis forced him to leave Bournemouth for a warmer climate. Years after she had left Bournemouth Flora was to write of her pilgrimages to his house:

> Skerryvore stands just as he left it. Memorial tablets to his pet dogs bear witness to his love for all living creatures. In their season, rhododendron blooms make vivid splashes of colour against the dark pines that once delighted his artist soul. From the upper windows may still be seen the glimpse of the sea that he delighted to point out to his guests. Only he, the life and soul of it all, has gone.[1]

Sadly the house too has gone now, damaged by a wartime bomb, it was pulled down and the site left as a memorial garden to Stevenson.

Flora's walks were soon curtailed, for in the autumn of 1903 her first child, a daughter was born, later to be christened Winifred Grace. Flora had no family support at this time. Her sister May had visited her in Bournemouth but the visits ceased before Winifred was born. Her parents were too far away for her mother to be with her for her confinement and her in-laws were on the Isle of Wight. The Thompsons did have friends, especially their next-door neighbours at No.6 Sedgley Road, Mr and Mrs Phillips. Mr Phillips was a pharmacist whose hobby was photography. It was he who took the photographs of Flora with her children. In later life she was said to have been averse to being photographed but perhaps she was happy to sit for Mr Phillips so that she could have photographs of her children. The results are certainly happier and more relaxed than studio portraits.

Winifred Thompson was christened on 7 August 1904, at St John's Church in Moordown, the next parish to Winton going out towards the country. At that time St John's was still a country church, although it was soon to be engulfed in the spreading streets of Moordown. Flora had grown up in the Anglican Church, strongly influenced by her Methodist grandfather, and later in life attracted to the Catholic church but she was to remain an Anglican and a regular worshipper. When she acquired her first radio in the 1920s she enjoyed listening to choral evensong broadcast in the afternoon. John Thompson's views on religion are not recorded, his politics were towards the left which may have meant that he was not a great supporter of the established Church but he was conventional enough to allow his children parish church christenings.

As a girl Flora had been apprehensive of handling babies so she had to develop confidence in her maternal abilities, she was much later to describe herself as a devoted mother but not a born nurse. She wrote of this time of her life: 'With a house to run single handed, with children being born and nursed my literary dreams faded for a while. But I still read a good deal. For the first time in my life I had access to a good public library and I slipped in like a duck slipping into water and read almost everything.'[2]

One of the great bonuses for Flora in living in Bournemouth was its excellent public library system. When she first lived in Winton the main library for Bournemouth was housed at Deane Park in the centre of the town some distance from her home. It was not a long walk by Flora's standards but her time was no longer her own. During her pregnancy and later with a baby to consider, trips to the library became rare treats. The lending libraries run by local shops cost money and much of their stock of light fiction was not to Flora's taste. She did discover a second-hand furniture shop in a side street, where among old cane-bottomed chairs and broken towel-horses was a box of smelly old books labelled 'Pick Where You Like 2d.'. Flora enjoyed looking through the boxes for readable books. She made many finds amongst the dry-as-dust residue of sermons and out-of-date guidebooks, and photography and stamp collecting manuals. But tuppences were not always easily spared from her housekeeping. Winton did have an old reading room with newspapers and some books, but when Flora had lived in Winton for four years, a new branch library was built only a short walk from her home. The free library, opened in 1907, was a joy to her, being well stocked and near at hand.

The great surge in library building in England all took place in Flora's lifetime. Mechanics' Institutes which had been Flora's first source of borrowed books began in 1808 to lend books to working men, but after the Jubilee in 1887 new public libraries opened at the rate of sixteen or more a year throughout the country.

Bournemouth opened its first public library in 1893 and from the beginning allowed open access to the shelves. In many other libraries readers had to make a request for a book to the librarian who brought their book from shelves behind the counter, browsing was not encouraged. Bournemouth's was only the second library in England to allow its readers open access to the shelves.

Although Flora was not able to write at this time, the reading she did was to enable her to write a long series of articles on writers and literary techniques within a few years. In the best Victorian tradition she was educating herself through her reading but with excitement and joy in her discoveries, not mere earnest endeavour. The free libraries of Bournemouth allowed her to add enormously to her knowledge of literature, they were her Open University.

Flora's interests kept her apart from her neighbours, except for a few kind friends she led a solitary life with only her baby for constant company. Other young wives spent all their physical and mental energies on keeping up appearances, endlessly dusting and polishing their unused front rooms. Flora cared more for a jug of wild flowers on the table than for a well-tended aspidistra in the window. The lives of many women of her class were monotonous, long lonely days full of repetitive domestic tasks, their leisure hours filled by embroidery or playing that great Edwardian status symbol, the piano. One of Flora's early articles for a newspaper was to be called 'The Silent Piano'. In it she wrote of the futility of non-musical families owning an expensive piano, which often served only as a surface on which bric-à-brac was displayed. She suggested that pianos could be sold to buy something which the family could really enjoy. She wrote:

> Are you a book lover, fill the blank space with a good bookcase filled with your favourite authors. Perhaps your tastes are artistic, a very small portion of that idle money would adorn your walls with good pictures. Are you a trade union or guild secretary, think of the hours of tedious labour a secondhand typewriter would save you. Don't keep a piano there silent and idle any longer. Turn it into something – anything of real worth and service to yourself and those you love.[3]

Such housewifely heresy seemed decidedly strange to many of the Thompsons' neighbours. Her taste in furniture too was different, she disliked the modern fashion for matching suites, preferring odd, interesting things. With enough money she would have been an antique collector, instead she used her innate good taste to help her to furnish her home in a style which was distinctly her own. She had a liking for books, old china and the colours green and white in conjunction. There were no embroidered antimacassars on Flora's chairs, she remained a poor seamstress but she did knit.

She had been taught by her mother and was a proficient knitter by the age of eleven when she began to knit her own stockings. During the Boer War women had knitted the socks, scarves and Balaclava helmets which soldiers had discarded all over the hot South African veldt. Flora too had knitted a long scarf of which she wrote: 'If anyone had told her how many miles of knitting she would do in her lifetime and what a great solace it would become to her she would not have believed them.'[4]

With a baby and a husband to knit for she always had something to do in the evening when she was not mending or reading.

Her life at this time must have been very humdrum. There are conflicting stories of the Thompsons' marriage. John has had a bad press from some who remember him as domineering, as a young husband he seems not to have entirely understood that he had married a girl of unusual sensibility and talent, but if he found her love of books and her desire to be a writer incomprehensible, that was the only way in which most men of his class and education would have reacted. His mellowed responses in later life say much for his character but in the early years of their marriage there were difficulties, as there often are when two different people must learn to adjust to one another.

In 1907 Edwin Timms left the army and came home from India. He had always wanted to work on the land so he went back to live with his parents and worked on a local farm. Two years as a farm labourer in Oxfordshire, where the wages of agricultural workers were the lowest in England convinced him that he must look for a better life. Edwin was already thirty and single, he had seen Africa and India and much as he loved Oxfordshire he knew that he could never make a good living at home, so he planned to emigrate to Canada. In 1909 he was ready to leave. Flora could not bear to let her best-loved brother emigrate to the other side of the world without seeing him for one last time. She decided to go home for a short holiday to see her parents and Edwin. It was not easy for her to get away from Bournemouth, John had to be left to fend for himself, six-year-old Winifred had to travel with her and to make things more difficult, Flora was expecting her second child. It was a journey of 100 miles from Bournemouth to Juniper Hill but it was a journey Flora was determined to make.

The train took Flora and Winifred to the nearest station to Juniper Hill, Aynho just inside the Northamptonshire border. There they got off the train at the small station which still stands, now derelict, by the Oxford canal. There Flora hired a pony and trap with a driver to take them on to Juniper Hill. The drive from the station up the long hill to Aynho village, took them past fields stripped to stubble, it was early autumn and the harvest was being gathered. Flora felt immediately at home again among the cornfields. Winifred was to remember that drive for a lifetime.

As they entered the pretty village of Aynho she saw that each cottage had a fruit tree trained on its walls, hanging with ripe golden fruit. Winifred who was not a country child asked her mother what the fruit were, Flora told her that the trees were apricots, planted by a tree-loving squire whose gardeners helped to maintain them and who would accept apricots in lieu of cottage rent. There are other stories of the origins of the Aynho apricots. One of them claims that Charles I or his son, stayed at Aynho Park and desired apricots which were unobtainable, so his host later ordered that sapling apricot trees be planted against all the cottages. Whatever the truth of the story, Aynho is called the apricot village of England, and at the right time of year, the ripe golden fruit can still be seen hanging from the trees trained on cottage walls just as Winifred Thompson remembered them.

Flora and her daughter both enjoyed the gentle ride which took them through the autumn countryside into Oxfordshire. Juniper Hill had changed little since Flora had left home and Winifred loved the cluster of houses surrounded by fields. The end house, where they were greeted on their arrival, had not changed much either but many of the children who had grown up in it had left. Flora had not seen her brother since he left to fight in South Africa. Winifred had never met her uncle or her grandparents, Albert and Emma Timms both then in their late fifties. Flora had to wait until the evening to see her beloved brother when he came home late from the harvest fields. Winifred left a picture of Edwin as she remembered him on this the only occasion she was ever to meet him, 'He was very tall,' she wrote, 'fair and suntanned after much foreign service and was very sweet to me as a small child.' Edwin had been back from India for two years, so his suntan probably owed as much to his work in the summer fields as to his foreign service.

Edwin was not the only one of Flora's family trying to make a living on the land and finding it difficult. Her younger brother Frank, then twenty-one was soon to emigrate to Australia where he became a successful fruit farmer in Queensland. Frank, like most of the hamlet men had a nickname, his was 'Fisher', because when anyone wanted him, his mischievous reply would be, 'I'm going fishing'. During the Second World War Flora and her sisters were to be very grateful for the parcels of food Frank was able to send to them. In the wartime Britain of food shortages, Australian tinned pears and peaches were a welcome luxury and a happy reminder of their fruit farmer brother. Most of the families Flora had grown up with, the Blabys, the Peverells, the Gaskins and the Blencoes, were still in the hamlet their sons struggling to live as farm workers, the younger ones among them were soon to die in the Great War.

Many of the old people Flora had known had died. Old Sally was dead and her cottage decaying, unwanted by young couples who did not care for thatched roofs and stone floors. Flora was sad to find little left of the snug home she had known with its thick walls and shutters, padded inside with Sally's red curtains and rag rugs. She wrote: 'The roof had fallen in, the yew hedge had run wild and the flowers were gone, excepting one pink rose which was shedding its petals over the ruin.'[5]

Queenie too had died in Bicester workhouse where she had been taken when housekeeping was beyond her. Though she had had one last day of glory. When King Edward VII was crowned in 1902, Queenie was fetched out of the workhouse and chaired through the streets of Bicester because she had lived through four reigns, and had been married on the day of Queen Victoria's coronation.

Old people in Juniper Hill had just acquired pensions when Flora visited the hamlet. Lloyd George's pensions of five shillings a week for the over-seventies, were first paid out in January 1909, so Flora saw the hamlet community briefly as the welfare state was being born. Flora never missed an opportunity to observe and record moments in time unnoticed by most people. One day she watched an early butterfly trying its newly opened wings and she remembered seeing one Friday morning:

> The old people of the place intent upon drawing their old-age pensions while the sunny weather lasted. As the butterfly fluttered past, first one, then another old man or woman would set down basket and umbrella to grab at the insect as it floated above them. One or two of the more active even attempted a chase, but the butterfly had easily the best of it, and dipped suddenly over a high wall, leaving a group of flushed and panting old folks to laugh together over their temporary loss of dignity.[6]

Flora was already storing in her memory what was changing before her eyes, her acute powers of observation sharpened by adult understanding. Social history was in the making, but only a few in every generation have Flora's ability to see, to understand and to record events. There is no shortage of contemporary reporting of the political events in 1909 and of the activities of the militant suffragettes who made the headlines. It took people like Flora Thompson and George Sturt, to notice the small details of rural life, so apparently insignificant and yet in retrospect, so very revealing of the slow but irrevocable changes going on in society.

During her holiday Flora did not see as much of Edwin as she would have liked, he was working such long hours in the fields, harvesting from first light until dusk. Horse-drawn reaper binders were in use then but men were still needed. Flora's brothers had grown up during the time when mechanization was increasingly used on farms. In the nineties they had both worked on the steam traction engines which, two to a field, pulled a plough backwards and forwards across the land on a cable. They had been part of the first generation of modern farm workers and were the first to suffer from the consequent decline in rural employment.

Flora and Edwin did have one long evening walk together, after they had walked to Brackley to see a younger sister off at the station. They prolonged their walk home in the September night so that they could talk, it was to be the last time they would ever spend together. Forty years later when Flora recorded their conversation, she called the first draft of the book in which it appeared, *Edmund*, the name she gave to Edwin in all her books, though it was as *Heatherley* the book was eventually published. In the original text of *Edmund* she records her last conversation with her brother, calling him Edmund and herself, as always, Laura:

> They stood talking of this and that, how York Minster and the Taj Mahal were the sights which had most impressed Edmund on his travels. Laura liked best of what she had seen, the new public library at Bournemouth, not so much as a building, as because of the books which were housed there. How she wished Edmund could have shared her joy in them.[7]

Edwin told his sister how he longed to farm in England, in his home county for preference, but without capital it was impossible, as a labourer he was not paid a living wage so he must emigrate. They stood in the darkness listening to a voice singing in the distance, one of the men they knew, singing on his way home, Flora recorded the point in time as it remained in her memory:

> It was but a popular song of the moment, but he had a pleasant voice and distance and the warm darkness lent enchantment. The brother and sister stood listening and savouring the earthy smells of the field in silence, then, as they turned to go, Edmund said, waving his hand to include the fields and trees and hedgerows both knew so intimately, 'I've seen a good bit of the

world but this takes some beating.' The next day Laura left for home and her brother sailed for Canada a week later.[8]

Although Edwin was to return to England briefly after five years in Canada, he and Flora were never to meet again.

8 Kitchen-table Writer

Flora's second child a son, Henry Basil, was born on 6 October that year, 1909. With two children to care for her literary ambitions remained unfulfilled for a short time longer. In the nature essays she was soon to write, she describes an incident in the life of a female ant preparing to make a home for the coming generation:

> The first thing she does is to nip off her own wings lest she should be tempted to disport herself in the sunshine, to the detriment of her maternal duties. There is something very human in this action, as many of my readers who are mothers will understand.[1]

It was this period of her life which gave Flora so much insight into the lives of women, particularly those with children. Flora was a devoted mother to her small daughter and baby son but she was determined not to sacrifice everything to motherhood like the female ant. She struggled to keep up her reading, which was deepening her knowledge of literature all the time and was soon to give her her first opportunity to appear in print. In her own words she was already ' ... working hard to educate herself, reading and writing, and how she loved the latter; loved the thrill of mastery when, after long trying, she succeeded in shaping some elusive thought into words.'

In 1909 John and Flora moved house again. They had already moved once, from No.4 to No.6 Sedgley Road when their friends Mr and Mrs Phillips moved out to a larger house in Stanfield Road. John and Flora's third home in Bournemouth was No.2 Edgehill Road, Winton, where they were to live for six years.

They called the house Grayshott Cottage. It was a pleasant house with a small garden and by all the standards of the day Flora was going up in the world. From her childhood in a cottage with a privy in the garden and no running water, she had moved to Edwardian mod. cons., but in fact she looked back on her life without luxuries with regret. In *Candleford Green* she was to describe the deep hot baths she had as a teenager in the old brewhouse in Fringford and compare them with:

> Those baths of later years when she stepped into or out of a few inches of tepid water in her clean but cold modern bathroom, or looked at the geyser ticking the pennies away and wondered if it would be too extravagant to let it run longer. But perhaps the unlimited hot water did less to make the brewhouse baths memorable than the youth, health and freedom from care of the bather.[2]

So Flora was not entirely happy. Her neighbours were proud of their hygienic bathrooms, their front rooms and bedrooms filled with matching suites whereas Flora missed the rag rugs and geraniums of Juniper Hill and the oak and willow pattern of Fringford. She found herself the odd one out in a highly conventional stratum of society and she longed to find a way to achieve her literary ambitions and to capture on paper her memories of what was fast vanishing from the land.

In 1910 Flora began to take a magazine called *The Ladies Companion* which cost one penny. It was an earnest magazine with articles on self-improvement and stories, aimed at lower-middle-class women. The magazine ran a book club for readers, encouraging women to read both the classics of English literature and living writers like Kipling, Belloc and Chesterton. The book club also ran literary competitions for the readers who sent their entries to Johnson's Court off Fleet Street, where they were judged by the club editor who used the pseudonym

Dorothea. After studying a few issues of the magazine Flora itched to enter one of the competitions, but then John was ill with 'catarrhal appendicitis'. Since Edward VII's appendicitis it had become the diagnosis of choice for all abdominal ills. John was away from work for almost two weeks during which time Flora had to be nurse as well as housekeeper, cook and mother and she had never enjoyed nursing.

John was at that time a member of the United Kingdom Postal Clerks Association, he probably held office in the local branch, as secretary perhaps, he was certainly a delegate to at least two national conferences. Flora's suggestion in her 'Silent Piano' article that a trade union or guild secretary would find a typewriter more use than a piano, makes it seem likely that John allowed her to have a typewriter, on condition that she typed the minutes of his meetings. Whenever Flora acquired her typewriter she soon taught herself to be very proficient in its use. Unlike John who wrote a good clear hand, Flora did not have good handwriting, and although handwritten manuscripts were still acceptable to editors she wanted to produce professional typescripts.

In February 1911, Dorothea of *The Ladies Companion* announced that the next competition was to be for the best essay on Jane Austen. For a lover of Jane Austen's work like Flora, the subject was one which she could not resist. Somehow she managed to find the time and the mental energy to write, despite having a lively one-year-old son to keep an eye on. Within the limit of 300 words she had to encapsulate her understanding of Jane Austen's success.

In the issue of *The Ladies Companion*[3] which came out on 25 February 1911 the winner of the competition was announced as Flora Thompson, Grayshott Cottage, Winton, Bournemouth. Flora's pleasure can be imagined. Her prize was any book or books up to the value of five shillings, a prize she enjoyed choosing, but the real prize was the boost to her morale at seeing her name in print for the first time. Dorothea liked her essay well enough to print most of the short article for readers to enjoy. These are the first of millions of Flora's words which were to appear in magazines over the next thirty years:

Before Jane Austen began to write, the novelists of her day had depended on involved plot, sensational incident, and the long arm of coincidence; therefore when these quiet, gentle stories appeared, dealing with everyday people and events, the public did not immediately recognise her genius or appreciate the gentle sarcasm that plays around her characters. It is true that her genius was at once recognised by a few of the greatest men and women of her time. Sir Walter Scott admired her work exceedingly, so did Sydney Smith, the Countess of Morley and, strange to say, the Prince Regent. She found, indeed, her own public of devoted admirers, but was then as now 'caviare to the general'. ... Jane Austen compared herself to a painter on ivory, and the enjoyment of her work is something like the possession of an exquisite miniature. Those who appreciate her art consider no praise too high. Those who do not, simply wonder how anyone can wade through the dull, tame pages, for no one loves Jane Austen moderately.

Flora was thirty-five, a self-taught writer and a largely self-educated woman. Her extensive reading enabled her to discuss a subject like Jane Austen intelligently. She researched her essay by finding every book referring to Jane Austen which Bournemouth's libraries could supply. She certainly referred to *A Memoir of Jane Austen* by J.E. Austen-Leigh, published in 1870, which detailed the admiration Sir Walter Scott, Sydney Smith, The Countess of Morley and the Prince Regent had for Jane. No doubt Dorothea also liked her appropriate quotation from *Hamlet*, 'the play I remember pleased not the million; 'twas caviar to the general'. Flora's assessment of Jane Austen's art is discerning, well researched and succinct enough to comply with the competition's word limit.

Once started, Flora kept writing entries for the book club competitions. On 1 April her essay on Emily Brontë won joint second prize and despite not being the winner, it was considered good enough to print in the magazine.

In the middle of April John took three days leave to attend a union conference. Left at home with the children Flora was able to have a holiday, with fewer meals to cook and less work to do in the house she took the children to the New Forest, a short train ride from Bournemouth. Flora loved the forest, one of her earliest published short stories opened with an arrival at a New Forest station.

He stepped from the primitive platform through a wicket gate, and the green peace of the forest closed upon him. There was no other building in sight, the road to the village wound between banks where the last primroses lingered with the first bluebells.[4]

Flora was no longer free to walk twenty miles as she would have done on her own, but she now had the pleasure of showing the forest, with its paths and heaths and ponies to her children. She found a magic in the forest which she was to use as background for stories for years to come. In an unpublished novel she recounted a picnic with the children.

> In the deserted apple orchard they found an open space of rabbit nibbled turf surrounded by bracken. There they made a crackling fire of gorse twigs, boiled their kettle and spread their cloth. After scones and cream the children crept into little houses, as they called the green caves supported on slender stalks beneath broad spreading bracken fronds.[5]

At the end of April she gained a mention for an essay on Catherine of Aragon, for whom she felt great sympathy. Flora liked to imagine that she was related to the only member of parliament who had had the courage to vote against the divorce of Catherine of Aragon. The member's name was Tems, a common name in the Thames valley. Flora believed that the Tems family became the Timms family of masons and boat builders from which her father was descended.

All Flora's efforts in 1911 went into her entries in *The Ladies Companion* competitions. In July she won first prize again, this time the subject was Shakespeare's heroines and Flora wrote about Juliet. Her essay, which was printed in full, opened with a descriptive piece of scene setting:

> The very name of Juliet calls up a vision of the Capulet's garden in old Verona, of those glimmering midsummer nights, when the wandering wind came laden with the heavy perfume of jessamine and tuberose and the nightingale sang all night in Juliet's pomegranate tree.[6]

Interestingly on the same page as Flora's essay, another prize was won, on the subject 'Six English Writers Most Sympathetic To Children', by someone called Cissy Ford of Heather Cottage, Bengal Road, Winton. Bengal Road adjoins Edgehill Road where Flora was then living. It may be pure coincidence that another woman was entering the competitions from the same part of Bournemouth, but it would be nice to think that at this time Flora had a friend with whom she could share her love of books. A friend involved in the same creative activity, would have been greatly valued by Flora, who did not make friends easily. She was by nature a loner but when she did make friends she was very loyal to them and her friendship was valued; as late as 1944 she was still writing to a friend in Bournemouth. There were more mentions of Flora's name in the book club results that year, she entered competitions on Thackeray, Shakespeare and Poetry versus Prose.

In the summer of 1911 John's mother died on the Isle of Wight and he took time off to go to her funeral. With the problems of ageing parents beginning to emerge, Flora must have been glad that some of her younger sisters were still close to home as she was so far away.

In January 1912 Flora had her first short story printed in *The Ladies Companion*. The editor already knew her name and her work, from her many competition successes, so she had plucked up the courage to send in a story. The story, called *The Toft Cup*,[7] appeared in the first issue of the New Year. In it, an old lady and her granddaughter are saved from penury by the discovery of a valuable old cup in their attic. It is a charming, romantic story and in its New Forest winter setting Flora was continuing to develop her descriptive powers, as in this passage from the story:

> During the night the frost had cast its spell over the woods and glades of the New Forest. This morning every branch and twig was hung with a pearly coating of hoar frost. Over the narrow lane by which the two women had come, the morning star glittered coldly. The silence of the winter dawn was only broken by the crop crop of a forest pony as it picked its scanty breakfast on the heath beside the road.

Flora was already learning to cast her spells too. The story was well constructed and if the characters are not strong, they do live. Flora was once told that she loved places more than people, the challenge made her uncomfortable but she had to admit its truth, it was a characteristic she was to use to her advantage once she abandoned fiction. Already in her first story her ability to describe was evident:

The sun had risen into a sky of brightest deepest blue, and the forest sparkled as though every bough was hung with myriads of diamonds. Every spray of bracken and blade of grass was sharply outlined with the exquisite tracery of frost crystals.

Perhaps there was just a touch too much purple in her ink, a few too many adjectives, but Flora was already honing her use of words, so that in time it was to be a sharp and true as the scythes of the harvest fields. The first echoes of *Lark Rise*[8] could be heard in that story which closes with the old lady telling her bees the news of a wedding in the family. Flora remembered all the folklore of beekeeping from her old neighbour Queenie at Juniper Hill, where bees were always told of marriages, births and deaths.

Flora received her first real payment for this story, it was a triumph for her persistence and determination. The sums she earned were small but a very welcome addition to John's wages and Flora was determined to earn enough to secure for her children a better education than she had had herself. For the next two years she regularly sent stories to magazines; many appeared in *The Ladies Companion*. Most of the stories were romantic but their romanticism has to be viewed in the light of the standards of the time, when much romantic verse was published and magazines like *The Strand* carried stories which were very sentimental by modern standards.

All Flora's stories written at this time had a rural background, most of them were set in the New Forest. Flora's favourite subjects had begun to appear, farms and farmers, gipsies and country craftsmen, though she lacked the courage to write about the rural poor. Perhaps if she had read George Bourne's *Change in the Village*[9] which was published in 1912, she might have written about Juniper Hill. However, despite their sentimentality, her stories gave Flora the opportunity to develop her writing style and their appearance in print gave her confidence in her ability to write.

9   Watershed

In 1912 the *Titanic* sank after hitting an iceberg, 1,513 people
died. Everyone was shocked that such a ship, the product of a
great industrial nation, should be lost on its maiden voyage.
Someone who expressed his feelings in print was the poet
Ronald Campbell Macfie. He wrote an ode on the sinking of the
Titanic which was published in the *Literary Monthly*.[1] The
magazine then ran a competition for readers who were to send
in their criticism of the ode. Flora decided to try this literary
competition: she won first prize.

Winning the competition was more than a boost to Flora's
morale, for it brought her into contact with the man who was to
be her friend and literary mentor for almost thirty years. Dr
Macfie wrote to Flora to express his personal appreciation of her
critique of his work and later came to see her in Bournemouth
unannounced. When they met Flora was thirty-six and Dr
Macfie forty-seven. He was a very attractive man, well educated
and a successful poet. In a correspondence years later on the
subject of pleasures Flora was to write:

> I personally shall never forget a couple of hours spent over a tea
> table with a poet whom I had only known so far by his published
> works. Such occasions in life are few but if we could choose our

company from our books there could be no better holiday than to
talk the sun down.

Flora and Dr Macfie were not able to talk the sun down, they
had only a few hours before Flora's domestic responsibilities
reclaimed her attention. Dr Macfie had a living to earn too, but
his brief visit was one of great importance to a kitchen-table
writer like Flora.

Ronald Campbell Macfie was a Scottish physician and writer.
He had qualified in medicine in Aberdeen in 1897 and
specialized in the treatment of tuberculosis. His medical career
coincided with the heyday of sanitoria which were being built all
over England and the Continent. In his forties Ronald Macfie
was earning his living as a resident medical officer in sanitoria, a
job which paid his bills and left him time in which to write. He
told Flora that he had renounced domestic life so that he could
remain free to write. Because his job provided him with a place
of residence, he was able to move from one hospital to another
as the fancy took him, and most of the best-known sanitoriums
had had his services as resident or locum medical officer.
Ronald Macfie's writings were not confined to literature, he
wrote many books on tuberculosis, hygiene and popular
medicine with titles such as, *Heredity, Evolution and Vitalism* and
The Romance of Medicine. He had also collaborated with Lady
Margaret Sackville in writing two books of fairy tales published
in 1909 and in 1912, the year in which he met Flora.

Lady Margaret Sackville was the daughter of the Earl de la
Warr, related to the Sackville West family and a writer of fairy
stories and much verse. She was six years younger than Flora,
very beautiful and very aristocratic. Dr Macfie was a
good-looking bachelor whom many literary ladies found
fascinating.

Ronald Macfie was a complex character, a poet, philosopher,
a man of enthusiasms and a supporter of causes. He was an
intensely religious man, his politics were those of a conservative
pacifist with radical leanings. A friend summed him up as, 'a
high strung breezy nature, loving much, fighting well, dreaming
dreams and helping his fellow men, he was very gentle, very
fierce, a devotee of beauty and a defender of the faith'. He was
everything that John Thompson was not; although Flora did not
want a substitute for her husband and Dr Macfie numbered

many more beautiful and talented ladies than Flora amongst his friends, but she was a lonely and ambitious writer who needed a literary friend. Ronald Macfie was a supporter of causes and Flora became one of his causes. It is significant that in story after story which Flora wrote, she supported friendship between men and women 'sexless, selfless friendship' which is what her relationship with Dr Macfie seems to have been.

Ronald Macfie had a list of published poems to his credit when he met Flora, and at that stage of her career she longed to be a poet instead of a writer of articles and romantic stories: he nourished her ambition. They kept up a correspondence and he would arrive on her doorstep, sometimes unannounced, whenever he could; his letters and his visits giving her great encouragement, though as it turned out, encouragement in the wrong direction.

Like Thomas Higginson encouraging Emily Dickinson in America fifty years earlier, Dr Macfie recognized talent when he saw it, although his judgement of the way in which it should be used was off course. Thomas Higginson had a genius on his hands and he failed to see that his advice to Emily Dickinson to regularize her highly original style was wrong. Ronald Macfie encouraged Flora to write verse, when what he was dealing with was an emerging writer of pure prose. Flora's genius may not be on a par with that of Emily Dickinson's but, as a writer, her need was the same, the confidence to cultivate her own original voice. Amongst Ronald Macfie's own poems is this one. The lady to whom it is dedicated may be any one of his female friends, his poems testifying to his many romantic friendships, but it could equally have been dedicated to Flora, who he called his poet friend.

To a Lady Who Sent Verses to Correct
    Erratic the metre
    And errant the rhyme
    The form might be neater
    And feater the time.
And yet thy sweet verses could hardly be sweeter,
    Though polished the metre
    And perfect the rhyme.

    I will not correct them
    As though they were prose

To carve and dissect them
Were rending a rose.
Thy charm and thy beauty preserve and protect them,
I will not correct them
As if they were prose.[2]

In 1913 Flora sold a story called *The Leper*[3] to *The Literary Monthly*, the magazine which had published Dr Macfie's *Titanic Ode* and her prize-winning essay on it. To have a short story published by a monthly literary magazine was a step up from working for the women's weeklies and *The Leper* is a romance of a very different sort. The story is set in medieval times on the Isle of Wight, when a young husband infected with leprosy is banished to a monkish cell in the woods. The story is much in the mould of the popular 'Roadmender Series', which included three of Edward Thomas's books. The series took its title from *The Roadmender* by Michael Fairless who also wrote the medieval romances, *The Gathering of Brother Hilarius* and *The Grey Brethren*, at a time when Celtic Twilight stories were in fashion. Michael Fairless was the pen name of a woman writer Margaret Barber who died in 1901 and Flora's story *The Leper* is very much in her style. Interestingly Flora set her story at Quarr Abbey near Ryde where her husband was brought up on the Isle of Wight and gave her hero the name Humphrey Stainer. Stainer was the maiden name of John Thompson's mother. Flora knew the island well, her husband's family all lived there, many still do and it was an easy journey to the island from Bournemouth.

Early in 1914 John took his family to the Isle of Wight to see his widowed father in Ryde. Flora recorded how on a day of showers and sunshine she stood alone on a low wooded hill:

All around and as far as I could see were primroses, primroses springing from the turf at my feet, breaking into foam at the edge of the clearing and yellowing the land right down to the little grassy fields which fringed the cliffs. A light shower had just fallen, and the scent of the flowers was indescribably fresh and sweet. As the sun reappeared a cuckoo began to call from a tree close by, and as I straightened my back from flower picking to listen, I saw a rainbow spanning the steeples of Ryde in a perfect arch. It was one of those rare moments which live in the memory forever.[4]

That was the spring of 1914, the last spring before the Great War, which was to alter the lives of a whole generation and alter society's attitude to women. Those attitudes had been slow in changing and John Thompson, like most men of his time, was reluctant to see change. He did not entirely approve of Flora's writing and it is not difficult to see why. Keeping one's self to one's self, was an important tenet of Edwardian life. Married women were supposed to conduct their lives modestly behind their parlour curtains, to have one's name in newspapers or magazines was to court notoriety and members of the Civil Service, however humble, were supposed to be circumspect.

Like most men of his era John Thompson was feeling threatened by the emancipation of women and the anarchic activities of the suffragettes. Flora had feminist sympathies and she did attend the meetings of the Women's Suffrage Movement in Bournemouth. She would have liked to have played a more active part in their campaign, but with two small children to care for she did not feel free to be an activist. If she had done, John would have been very shocked. However, Flora's support for the suffragettes remained very strong, she once wrote:

> The vote, once secured for her sex would make women the equals of men in prestige and opportunity. Women's position in the home too, would be a very different one when she was armed to fight for her own and her children's welfare.[5]

In a lighter vein but with the same underlying theme, Flora later wrote about the adoption of the bicycle by women and quoted a popular verse of the day:

> Mother's out upon her bike enjoying of the fun,
> Sister and her Beau have gone to take a little run,
> The housemaid and the cook are both a-riding on their wheels
> And Daddy's in the kitchen a-cooking of their meals.

She went on to comment wryly, 'and very good for Daddy it was. He had had all the fun hither to, now it was his wife's and daughter's turn. The knell of the selfish, much waited upon, old fashioned father of the family was sounded by the bicycle bell.'[6]

Flora may not have had a bicycle but she did have her typewriter and was quietly working away at a measure of liberation for herself, as she put it: 'the right to use my scant leisure as I wished'.

But John kept a strict hold on his family's lives where he could. Norman Phillips, the son of the pharmacist neighbour who took Flora's photograph, asked if Winifred could join The League of the Helping Hand, a children's organization run by a national newspaper. Flora had to tell him that her husband would not allow it as the newspaper was owned by Alfred Harmsworth, later Lord Northcliffe. Presumably Harmsworth's right-wing views did not suit John who was a Liberal.

War with Germany was declared in August 1914. At first Flora was not immediately affected, her husband at thirty-nine, was not expected to fight, her son was too young and her best-loved brother was safe in Canada. Ronald Macfie was to have some strange adventures during the war but he was too old to serve as an army doctor.

Flora was beginning to tire of writing romantic stories. In 1915 *The Ladies Companion* magazine ceased publication, the mood of the times was not right for romance. In later years she wrote of her early stories: 'it was not of writing small sugared love tales that I dreamed in my youth'.[7] Flora's stories had not been poorly written or meretricious but her integrity had been a little compromised by the sentimental standards of pre-war days. The stories were not worthy of a Jane Austen disciple, but then Jane never needed money as Flora did.

In 1915 the Thompsons moved again, into the neighbouring Frederica Road where they occupied No.42 which again they called Grayshott Cottage. Like all their Bournemouth homes, it was a typical suburban house for a white-collar worker on a modest salary. A solid detached house under a gabled roof; millions like it were being built on the outskirts of every town in England. It had bay windows at the front and a french window opening onto a small garden at the back. But a new house could not compensate for the unhappy times in which they were living.

War news was becoming worse, the 'It will be over by Christmas' attitude of 1914 had died in the trenches and Zepplin raids brought the reality of war home to those who still thought that war was an heroic adventure. Appeals began for women to do war work and for the first time women were openly encouraged to do dirty and dangerous jobs in industry, munitions and on the land. Flora could have returned to her old job as a Post Office assistant and telegraphist to release a man to fight, but she was thirty-eight, middle-aged by the standards of the day and had two children at home. Basil was only six and Winifred was twelve. A generation earlier, Winifred would have been expected to leave school to look after her small brother but attitudes were changing and Winifred was doing well at school. Flora wanted to maintain her journalistic output to help pay towards her children's schooling, so when *The Ladies Companion* closed down she wrote articles for newspapers and continued writing poems and short stories to sell.

Flora soon had the anxiety of a brother in uniform to bear. Edwin rejoined the army in Canada, he was to fight in the Eastern Ontario Regiment. He was given home leave before he was sent to France. Flora longed to go home to see him again. Despite censored news it was becoming obvious to everyone that a soldier's chance of survival at the front was decreasing daily. Edwin's home leave was granted in a wintry March, there was late snow and both of Flora's children had been ill with whooping cough, they were not fit for a long journey and she could not be spared from nursing them.

So Edwin left for France without seeing his sister again. He was sent straight to the front where he went into battle with his well-worn copy of Sir Walter Scott's poems in his pocket. Three weeks after leaving home he was killed.

The first Flora knew was when a morning's post included a letter of her own to Edwin, returned marked 'Killed In Action'. It arrived on a perfect spring morning in early April, when her spirits had been high because her children were better and she was looking forward to summer, when she could get out of doors again after a dark and difficult winter. Winifred remembered her mother's reaction to the news of Edwin's death: she was quite simply heartbroken. Edwin Timms was buried in Woods cemetery, Zillebeke in Belgium, his name was added to the list of ten other dead soldiers in Cottisford church. Flora had known them all as childhood companions.

The death of her brother was a watershed in Flora's life, it broke the last real links with her childhood. She was almost forty and her life was about to change again, the time for romantic dreams was over.

John Thompson became restless too and he decided to apply for a job which was advertised in the *Post Office Circular*. The job was that of salaried sub-postmaster of Liphook in Hampshire. It was a sensible move, to be a big fish in a small pond suited John's temperament and the family would be better off. Flora was pleased with the idea, she needed a change, something to help her to assuage her grief at Edwin's death. Liphook was within walking distance of Grayshott and the Hampshire countryside she loved so much. John got the job and in August 1916 became sub-postmaster of Liphook. Flora left Bournemouth and her modern house without regret, to move with her children into the house which adjoined the Liphook Post Office. It was summertime in Hampshire and a new era was beginning for Flora and her work.

10 The Bright Day

One of Flora's first long walks after the move to Liphook was complete, was a nostalgic pilgrimage to Grayshott. Early in September she walked through Bramshott and out on Rectory Lane, of which she was to say in the guide to Liphook she later wrote:

> When Marvell wrote of a green thought in a green shade he might well have been thinking of Rectory Lane Bramshott, for the banks 12 to 15 feet high on either side are draped with ferns and festooned with creepers, while the boughs of the beeches which crown them meet overhead so densely in places, that even the light filters greenly.[1]

The lane became a path which dipped down to Waggoners Wells, the chain of lakes Flora had loved in her Grayshott days. After the years in Bournemouth her walk was a delight, a return to much-loved haunts.

Flora found Grayshott little changed, the ambitious plans she remembered hearing for its development seemed to have come to nothing. Hindhead had grown and overtaken Grayshott in importance. If Grayshott had not changed by 1916, Flora had. She was within months of her fortieth birthday and already noticing a few grey hairs. In her book *Heatherley* she paints a portrait of herself at this time:

> She shared with other women of her age the extension, if not of youth of apparent youngishness due to recent revolutions in fashion. The long heavy skirts, the elaborately coiled hair, the fussy trimmings and loaded hats of pre-war days had disappeared and a simpler style had emerged. In a neat scantily cut costume with the skirt reaching but a little below the knee and a small plain hat worn over bobbed hair, many a woman of forty looked younger than she had done at thirty.[2]

The simplicity of these wartime fashions pleased Flora, particularly the shorter skirt, she was always too energetic a walker for long skirts. She retained a liking for good-quality classic clothes all her life and was remembered by those who knew her as a woman who dressed with good taste.

Her visit to Grayshott revived many memories, pleasant and unpleasant. Walking around Flora saw a few familiar faces, a shopkeeper, a local reporter she had once known well, but only in the teashop did she speak to anyone of having once lived in the village. She had the experience common to all who return to once-familiar places and find themselves strangers.

Before she returned home she stood for a moment in the evening sunlight, remembering her youthful self seeing the same scene for the first time, recalling too:

> The intervening years, crammed with the busy responsibilities, joys and anxieties, hopes and setbacks, inseparable from running a home and bringing up a family. Often for months together she had not been out of doors alone at a distance from home, as she was that evening. Now, standing apart though but a short space apart in time or distance from her loved home ties, she was able once again to think of herself as an individual.[3]

But first there was a Post Office in wartime to cope with. Liphook Post Office was short of staff and very busy with extra mail for the troops stationed nearby. Flora's war effort was to return to her old job.

Now that she lived in a house adjoining the Post Office, Flora could sort the morning mail and still be on hand to get the children off to school. She got up at four in the morning to sort the huge incoming mail. There were two large army camps near

Liphook, Longmoor and Borden camps, which greatly
increased the mail passing through the area. The middle years
of the war were a difficult time for everyone, food supplies were
becoming a problem, the government asked the nation to
undertake voluntary rationing with very little effect. Flora had
little time or energy for writing. After doing her four hours' mail
sorting work before breakfast and getting her children off to
school, she had to run the house, queue for food and try to make
meals for four people out of very little. Once she experimented
with a dish suggested in a newspaper article on wartime cookery,
it was a dish of stewed snails which she gathered and prepared
laboriously only to find that they tasted like stewed rubber.

As so often in wartime, people were permanently tired. John
Thompson spent nights sleeping in the Post Office on a camp
bed close to the telegraph machine, ready to take urgent
messages. The Thompsons had arrived in Liphook at a very
difficult time.

The Post Office spent over a hundred pounds repairing the
house in which the family lived. It must have been in need of
much renovation. It is a tall, rather gaunt house opening straight
off the street. New grates were put in the sitting rooms, and a
new 'kitchener', a type of range, in the kitchen. There was a box
room to spare which Flora furnished with a desk, a chair and a
wastepaper basket for herself. When she could snatch a few
moments from her various duties, it was there she went to write,
driven as she was later to say: ' ... by the feeling that in return
for the precious opportunity known as life some further effort
other than those involved in mere living were required of her.'[4]

She was still exchanging letters with Ronald Macfie who
continued to encourage her to write poetry. In the difficult war
years his letters always cheered her up: 'Forty, what is forty,' he
wrote in one letter. 'I am fifty one but if I could yet have ten
years of opportunity to write I should be content. Look forward,
rejoice in your great gift and fight for opportunity to use it even
if it be ten years later; and perhaps I who am still fighting may in
a few years be able to find some ways and means for you. Who
knows?'

But Dr Macfie had little real understanding of the problems
which are inherent in being a writer who is also a wife and
mother. He viewed the life of a poet in a lofty and romantic way:
it is surprising that down-to-earth Flora was not put off by

Cottisford Church where Flora worshipped as a girl

Old Queenie, the beewoman and
lacemaker, 1880

Cottisford School where Flora was a pupil in the 1880s, photographed in 1905

The forge and the post-office at Fringford in the 1890s with Mrs Kesia Whitton holding the horse's head

The men at the forge at Fringford in the 1890s

A girl telegraphist in the 1880s

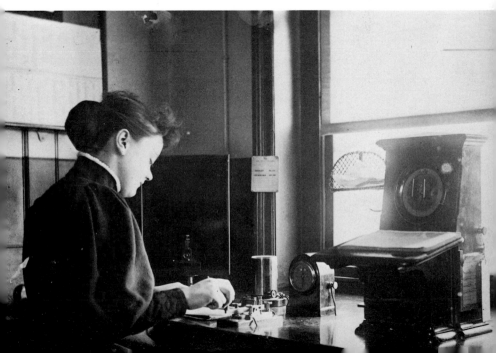

Flora's brother Edwin Timms photographed in India
in about 1905

Flora and her daughter in about 1905

Flora and her son in Bournemouth, 1911

Winton Library, Bournemouth today

Flora and John Thompson's home at Grigg's Green today

Liphook post-office during the First World War

Mildred Humble Smith, ten years before she and Flora ran the Peverel Society

Dr Ronald Campbell Macfie, Flora's 'beloved friend'

Flora at her typewriter in 1921

Flora Thompson's grave in Dartmouth

TO
THE DEAR MEMORY
OF
FLORA THOMPSON
MAY 21ST 1947

AND
OF HER BELOVED
YOUNGER SON
PETER REDMOND
THOMPSON
LOST AT SEA
SEPT. 16TH 1941.

Ronald Macfie's work. Elves and fairies peep from his pages of poetry in a way which makes a modern reader wince, but as late as 1922 Sir Arthur Conan Doyle was not afraid to declare his belief in fairies, so Macfie was perhaps only reflecting current tastes. He remained Flora's beloved friend.

Flora did have to fight to find time and energy for her writing. She longed for the end of the war, for her children to need her attention a little less, but then at the age of forty she found that she was pregnant again. It was the last thing that she and John wanted, although in time this last child turned out to be their best-loved. John Thompson in his middle years was a man who was strict with his staff, a typical civil servant, but at home a fairly happy family man. His tolerance of the time Flora spent at her desk was still uncertain, between them they ran a busy Post Office, a home and a family, and now there was to be another child.

1917 was a bad year for everyone, compulsory rationing came in limiting sugar, butter, margarine and meat. Street lamps were dimmed and every house had to cover its windows at night. There was a shortage of fuel as well as food, coal prices shot up as supplies diminished and housewives were forced to save clinkers and cinders to burn. It was a miserable time. Flora dreaded the long months of pregnancy, she was no longer young and had hoped that her days of childbearing were over. Her daughter was fifteen and her son nine, she had no stocks of baby clothes or equipment to use. There was everything to get again and at inflated prices, having a new baby put a great strain on the Thompsons' budget. Not even Ronald Macfie's encouragement could help Flora to overcome this crisis, the child would be born and she must care for it, her writing would have to wait.

The end of the Great War in 1918 coincided with the birth of Flora's second son who she called Peter Redmond, a curious choice of second name, which may indicate Flora's sympathy for the Irish cause then so much in the news. John Redmond, a devout catholic and active in the movement for Irish home rule died in 1918, his name was perhaps given to Flora's baby as a memorial.

Although the war was over, life was not to be back to normal for a long time. A virulent form of influenza, which was to kill more people than the war had done, swept across Europe. The disease soon arrived in England with the returning troops and hundreds of soldiers stationed near Liphook died. Hardest hit were the Canadian soldiers stationed at Bramshott where 300 men are buried in the small churchyard planted with maple trees in their honour. On her walks that autumn Flora noticed a particularly good crop of blackberries where the Canadian camp had been. Tens of thousands of men had drilled there on the heath and the brambles had been cut down to the earth, they also received a dressing of camp residue. After lorries had removed all the camp buildings, nature set to work to heal the scars. Flora wrote: 'Almost the first growth was the long shoots of blackberry brambles. The fruit when it followed, was of the finest – cultivated fruit indeed – cultivated at what tremendous cost.'[5]

Whilst the influenza epidemic lasted, Flora watched her two older children who could so easily have brought the fatal influenza home from school. John was vulnerable too, working long hours in contact with the general public. Flora nursed her new baby and longed for an end to the epidemic and a return to normal life.

No one in the Thompson family did catch influenza, though there was a family death soon after Peter's birth. Flora's father, Albert Timms died in December 1918, he was sixty-four. When he was buried in Cottisford on 17 December, Flora was in no position to travel to Oxfordshire, so it was left to her remaining brothers and sisters to support Emma, twice bereaved within two years. This role fell to Flora's sisters May, Betty and Annie. Betty was to see more of Flora in the years to come when she became a Post Office worker and an aspiring writer herself.

Slowly the epidemic waned but there was no rejoicing. Thousands of demobbed soldiers were without work and the women who had worked so hard in industry and on the land, were told to go back home. Without the impetus of patriotic duty to perform, men in industry began to voice their feelings about their poor treatment and pay, resentment was in the air and there were strikes and disturbances. The old settled order which Flora's generation had known was gone forever.

Flora's own life, however, gradually became easier. She no longer had to get up to sort the mail, the staff shortage was over now that men were returning to civilian life. Her two older children were both at good schools in the area, one at Petersfield the other Haslemere. Winifred was by then known to most people as Diana, a name she seems to have chosen for herself in preference to her own; Liphook people who knew her, still believe that Diana was her second baptismal name.

Flora had written very little during the years of war, and as her output had dropped so had her confidence. She solved this by answering an advertisement in the *Daily News* which offered a writing course. The course was run by the Practical Correspondence College in London. Correspondence courses for amateur writers were popular at that time: homebound women frequently tried to find their way into freelance journalism to gain a measure of independence and creative outlet. Few of the college's customers would have been as talented as Flora. One scrap of praise and advice on marketing her work remains amongst her papers. Although short, the praise is fulsome: 'This is really good. You have handled the situation with the mastery of genius. Please send to one of the magazines on the list. I am proud of this story, it does you the highest credit.'[6]

The praise is signed A. Brodie Frazer, the *Daily News*. A. Brodie Frazer was on the staff of the *Daily News* from 1915 to 1922 and possibly, like many journalists, he also freelanced as a correspondence-course tutor. If so, he either believed in encouraging his students with great praise, or he saw in Flora's work great promise. He probably suggested that *The Catholic Fireside* magazine would be a good outlet for her work, it may have been one of the magazines on the list which he mentioned. However she came to it, Flora was to succeed in selling work to *The Catholic Fireside* and soon became a regular contributor, remaining with them for over eight years.

The first story she submitted to *The Catholic Fireside* was 'The Leper' which had appeared in 1913 in *The Literary Monthly*. Flora altered the medieval romance slightly and it reappeared in January 1920. That year she wrote six stories for the magazine.

As a contributor to *The Catholic Fireside* she was in good company, E. Nesbit was also a contributor in 1920. The magazine was a mixture of stories, women's features on fashion and cookery, articles on gardening and some verse. Despite the fashion, the cookery and articles aimed at 'Catholic womanhood', the magazine also included articles which were frankly feminist in tone: features on finance, life insurance and education for women. Its slightly radical but at the same time, traditional values, appealed to Flora.

John's attitude to Flora's work at this time, when her output was increasing fast and being published, can be guessed from hints in her stories. In an undated, unpublished short story,[7] Flora wrote of a wife whose youthful ambition to be an artist revived when her children were older. The woman showed one of her new paintings to her husband who: ' ... laughed with amused tolerance and advised her to stick to fancy needlework!' Had John arrived at an amused tolerance? If so Flora had quite enough determination to survive amused tolerance, annoying as it must have been. The main obstacle to her work was always time. She had a small child and a husband who worked at home. John had an office in the house with a door through to the Post Office, so that he could keep a strict eye on his staff and customers. He was at home for lunch, a hindrance which Flora had not had in Bournemouth, but somehow she made time and her output was soon to double.

In June 1920 an article of Flora's appeared in *The Catholic Fireside* instead of a short story, it was entitled 'Skerryvore'[8] and was about Robert Louis Stevenson's home in Bournemouth, which Flora had known so well. It was the first time she had had a literary essay accepted since the days when she had entered the literary competitions in *The Ladies Companion*.

Of the short stories which Flora wrote in 1920 the most significant is one of the shortest, 'The Hermit's Yew' published in *The Catholic Fireside* in September 1920. The story is about the destruction of an ancient yew tree by the new owner of the land on which it stood. The landowner, a retired pork butcher who had profited from government contracts during the war, had also felled a lilac hedge, pride of the village, oaks and beeches in a wood and finally the venerated yew. An old man from the village, Mr Renshaw, pleaded for the felling to stop but:

> ... the work of destruction went on: the flowering bluebells were trodden underfoot to an unwholesome looking blue and green pulp. The wild cherry trees by the Butts gate came down with the rest, in all their snowy glory though they were. As Renshaw said his red old eyes watering, ' 'twer murder, nothing less'.[9]

Some of Flora's other stories at this time were still romantic but in 'The Hermit's Yew' she was addressing problems about which she cared deeply. There is no sentiment in the story and its theme of the need to protect the countryside from exploitation rings true. If Flora read Thoreau she must have been struck by his assessment of writers, in *A Writer's Journal* in 1841, he wrote, 'The best you can write will be the best you are. Every sentence is the result of a long probation. The author's character is read from title page to end. Of this he never corrects the proofs.'[10]

By the beginning of 1921 she submitted the first of her long series of nature articles to the editor of *The Catholic Fireside*. On 1 January her article, 'Out of Doors In January'[11] appeared. An 'Out of Doors' article was to appear each month of 1921. The twelve articles are set in the New Forest, and in them Flora adopted a middle class identity which was largely wish fulfilment. The writer purported to be a doctor's daughter living in a cottage in the forest. The home she created for herself was a dream, the characters, an actress friend and a catholic priest, actors on a stage set, but the rural scene was real.

There is evidence that at a later date, Flora herself wanted to remove the dream parts of these articles. A copy of one of them, now housed in the University of Texas, is anotated in her own hand and initialled where she has edited it, possibly when she was hoping to have the articles published in book form years later. Against one of the longest descriptions of her dream cottage she has written, 'please leave out'. The section she wanted to remove began:

> The front of the house is very old, as the oak cross beams and the heavy stone window frames testify, but the long low ceilinged parlour at the back was built on some time during the early part of the last century. This room is my real home. Here I have gathered together my books and pictures, the old writing table at which my father wrote out his prescriptions, my grandmother's blue and white china, and the samplers of my great aunts.

This is all pure fantasy which Flora later regretted but who can blame her for it? Reality was the house attached to a busy Post Office, full of family cares and domestic work.

Also in 1921 Flora collected together her poems and at Dr Macfie's instigation she found a publisher for them. The thin paper-bound book was entitled *Bog Myrtle and Peat*[12] and was dedicated to Dr Ronald Campbell Macfie. The book was advertised in *The Catholic Fireside* in May 1921: 'The author of these beautiful open-air poems is Post-Mistress in a small Hampshire village. Her verses make instant appeal to all who love the English countryside.'[13]

Winifred Thompson later recalled the amusing time the family had with reporters from local and national newspapers who came to interview her mother after the book was published. To Flora's embarrassment one of them called her 'The Postmistress Poet' in a report which ran:

> The people of Liphook have always believed that in the pleasant situation of their village and the natural beauties of their countryside, they had enough for proper local pride. Now they find that they possess a hitherto undiscovered, unsuspected poetess.

Flora did not enjoy her first brush with publicity but John and the children found it all most amusing. Flora kept well away from publicity after this.

The reviews of *Bog Myrtle and Peat*[14] were kind but the book was not successful. The verses do, however, reveal much about Flora, her preoccupation with the countryside and Dr Macfie, and her love for her brother Edwin whose loss was still fresh in her memory five years after his death. In a poem entitled 'August Again' she wrote:

> The heather flings her purple robe
>   Once more upon the hill;
> Beneath a shivering aspen-tree
>   My Love lies cold and still:
> Ah, very deep my Love must sleep,
>   On that far Flemish plain,
> If he does not know that the heath-bells blow
>   On the Hampshire hills again.[15]

Winifred Thompson wrote years later that Flora would not own *Bog Myrtle and Peat*[16] because she felt that it was not good enough. Winifred herself wished that her mother had continued to write poetry but said in a letter to a friend, 'I fear the life we led then was not conducive to her doing so.'

Flora was not happy in 1921. In July she wrote to a friend: 'I have been feeling very low and depressed and have got very behind with my work.' In the same letter she felt the need to lay claim to her tenuous connection with the Wallington family, writing: 'I am a great believer in heredity. My grandmother's family were aristocratic people, the late General Sir John Wallington was a cousin of hers and his son, who is now secretary to Queen Mary, would be a distant connection. They had one or two writers (undistinguished) in the family and I often wonder if this obscure writer in Liphook is a throwback to them.'[17]

Flora was almost in danger of falling into the trap which her father had created for himself. The failure of her first book was a blow to her emerging confidence, which she boosted by claiming socially elevated relatives. Luckily she had too much of her mother's common sense and her own moral fibre, to nurture resentment as her father had done. It is ironic that she was not to achieve lasting fame until, in old age, she admitted to her humble origins and used them in her books.

In 1922 Flora changed the style of her articles for *The Catholic Fireside*. Out went the affectations and the fictional middle-class character and in came more of her own acute observations of nature and the seasons. In this she was returning to her true spirit; even as a young girl she had known that her life's deepest joys would be in the delight of commonplace but lovely things.

The new-style articles had a new title too, 'The Peverel Papers'.[18] No one knows why the name Peverel was her choice, although she did admit that Peverel Down was her name for Weaver's Down, Liphook. Ideas have been put forward that she took the name from Peveril Point or Bradford Peverel in Dorset. A reader in the twenties asked if the village of Peverel near Devonport was her location, but it was a name she had known since childhood, there were Peverells in Juniper Hill, two Peverell brothers died in the Great War, their names are recorded above Edwin's on the war memorial in Cottisford church. She was also a lifelong lover of Sir Walter Scott's work: she and Edwin memorized it in great chunks and Edwin carried his book of verse into battle, so perhaps Peveril of the Peak influenced her liking for the name. Anything associated with her brother was important to her.

Whatever the source of their title, there were to be seventy-two Peverel Papers, one each month in *The Catholic Fireside* for the next six years.

It has been suggested that Flora's model for her nature writings was Gilbert White. Flora certainly knew and loved the work of this greatest of all English naturalists and emulated his patient and detailed methods of observation, but her style of writing was all her own.

To find material for 'The Peverel Papers' every month, Flora walked the woods and hills alone. Mr Joe Leggett who lived at Griggs Green in Liphook remembers as a boy meeting Flora when she was out on her walks, he writes:

> She was a familiar figure to me, who always seemed to appear in the remotest parts of Woolmer Forest, Weaver's Down, Bramshott Common, out towards Milland and around Waggoners Wells or Forest Mere. She often spoke to me as I roamed the wilderness looking for birds' nests. She had a kind authoritative voice imploring me not to disturb or rob the nests. … The people of Liphook were unable to arrive at a solution as to what made her walk the numerous paths, to stand gazing at whatever caught her eye, a bird in flight, foxes in a distant open space enjoying a gambol in the sun, a fallen tree or a farmer ploughing a field.[19]

The people of Liphook remained puzzled, for Flora was far too reserved and modest to tell them about her writing. Solitude was essential to her work, alone she could silently observe birds and wildlife and plan her articles. After twenty years of marriage and bringing up her family, she had regained the freedom of the fields and she began to be happy again.

Country bus services which began to run in the Liphook area, gave her much pleasure. One day when she boarded a bus on which every seat was full, the driver offered her a place beside himself behind the steering wheel. He then proceeded to do the honours by giving Flora a running commentary on the countryside as he drove through it. Flora was reminded of the old coaching days and the honours of the box seat. She wrote:

> We passed through the heart of the Gilbert White country, and within a mile of his own village of Selborne. The narrow lanes, with honeysuckles which brushed the bus windows, must often have seen that father of English nature lovers, jogging along on his sedate and steady-going grey mare.[20]

Bus rides enabled Flora to travel much further than she could on foot and in the limited time available to her, she loved them: 'The printed lists of places upon the routes chime like bells in the memory,' she wrote, 'Haslemere and Fernhurst; Milland and Forest Mere. What a line of good mouth-filling, ready-made poetry to be printed on the front of a bus.'[21] Every month new routes opened up and new places became accessible to Flora. She considered the country bus as delightful a feature of country life as the wild birds, because they lent wings to the wingless.

Flora received letters of appreciation from readers, she later wrote, 'from these I found that the feature most liked in the articles were sketches of old country life and characters remembered from my childhood and I determined that at some future time I would describe them more fully. The idea took shape in my mind that a book about my old home might please readers.' So Flora was thinking about writing of her childhood as early as 1922, but she had to serve another fifteen years' apprenticeship first: there were to be more stories, poems and articles, novels finished and unfinished, before *Lark Rise*[22] was born.

11   The Journalist

In 1923 Flora was forty-seven, Peter her youngest child started school and she had more time in which to write. To create a market for her increased output she persuaded the editor of *The Catholic Fireside* to let her begin a reader's circle called 'The Fireside Reading Circle', a literary feature like the 'Book Club' run by *The Ladies Companion* which had given Flora her first chance to appear in print. Flora adopted a similar format, although her essays on literature were much longer and more fully researched, some of them running to three or four closely printed pages of the magazine. Flora was not just a housewife dabbling in journalism by the mid 1920s but a hardworking and determined writer.

The Reading Circle was a project close to Flora's heart. Her knowledge of literature was already extensive but for these articles she had to read and research the works and the biographies of her chosen subjects; work she enjoyed very much, though she must have had some difficulties doing literary research whilst living in rural Hampshire. The articles still make good reading and leave one in no doubt that had she been able to study literature at university, Flora could have had a good academic career. For a woman whose elementary education finished at fourteen, the essays are a remarkable achievement.

The articles fall into groups, those about authors, Dickens, Scott, Keats, Wordsworth, Carlyle, George Eliot, the Brontës, Browning, Tennyson, Alice Meynell, Thackeray, Stevenson, Rossetti, Ruskin, Meredith, Conrad, Patmore, Bennett, Kipling, Chesterton, Barrie; and those about groups of writers, for example women poets and nature poets. Then there were general studies of English literature such as 'The Evolution of the Novel', 'The English Short Story', 'Atmosphere in English Literature'; the list is long and impressive.

Many of these literary features throw light on Flora's view of her own work, for example in her piece on 'English Essayists' she writes:

> Special qualities are required of the essayist. A poem or a novel may spring from the inner consciousness of an author: a certain degree of art is, of course necessary to develop either ... but the essay is never inspired in the sense that the poem or story may be; reasoning powers must be brought to reinforce imagination to make an essayist.[1]

Flora certainly had both reasoning and imagination. There were to be two pieces on essayists, in which Flora wrote of the work of Francis Bacon, Sir Thomas Browne, Dryden, Milton, Cowley, Addison, Jonson, Goldsmith, Sir Joshua Reynolds and Gilbert White. Such articles must have taken her weeks to research and write.

Like the old Book Club, The Fireside Reading Circle included writing competitions for its readers which Flora judged, her verdicts appearing in a subsequent issue of the magazine. Her desire to help amateur writers as she had been helped a decade earlier, is obvious. Both men and women entered the competitions, many of the women were nuns with whom she corresponded for years. All of the contributors chose a pseudonym which allowed Flora to criticize their work in print.

Whenever possible she was encouraging, often suggesting new forms that the less successful might try, poor poets were encouraged to try prose or drama, failed essayists guided towards letter writing. But occasionally she could suggest no remedy and was quite blunt; then the writer must then have been glad of their anonymity. An example is the contributor whose pseudonym was Morris, of whose work Flora wrote: 'I am afraid that your friend is prejudiced in your favour. None of the

pieces you sent me are poetry or even passable verse.'² Less
harsh but equally uncompromising was this to Georgia: 'I am
afraid you will have to throw in your lot with the mighty army of
readers, just as essential to literature as writers are.'

The competition subject was sometimes related to the
accompanying article or was more general, as when Flora chose
the title 'A Day In My Life',³ and had to persuade her readers
that things which seemed commonplace in their lives might be
of great interest to others. She came up against the problem
encountered by most teachers of creative writing, that of
would-be writers preferring to write about exotic lives and
places they can only imagine, whilst neglecting their own lives
which are full of interesting material. Flora's comments on the
results of this particular competition, tell us much about her
readers and her attitude to their lives and work. She wrote:

> The worldly circumstances of our competitors vary greatly. In
> some of the essays, music, art, walking or driving and games had
> a place in a typical day, other papers show lives full to
> overflowing with work and struggle, two of the women writers
> being not only homemakers but breadwinners, fathers and
> mothers in one. Between the two extremes come nuns living
> beautifully ordered lives in their convents, business men, a music
> teacher, a domestic help, three cotton workers, two florists, a
> confectioner and several housewives. Excepting to say how much
> sympathy I feel with the cares and aims of each, and the wonder
> and admiration with which I regard those doing seeming
> impossibilities – working all day in a cotton mill in one case then,
> while the copper boiled for a big wash at night, sitting down to
> write for our competition, I will use the space left in giving
> extracts from the essays. They will I am sure, prove more
> illuminating than any comments that could be made on them.

She was right to resist imposing her own comments on work
which spoke so eloquently for itself. Her touch was always sure
and her readers loved her for it, as countless readers of her
books were to do.

A young woman who entered her work in the competitions
was soon to become one of Flora's few close friends. Her name
was Mildred Humble-Smith, she was ten years younger than
Flora, a married woman with two sons, Anthony the youngest
and Roger who was the same age as Peter Thompson. Mildred,
or 'Myldrede' as she called herself in print, had had an easier

life than Flora. She was the daughter of a well-to-do ship's chandlers and nautical instrument makers family in Newcastle on Tyne. She married a man who had been in the Brazilian navy although he was from a family of English surgeons and dentists. Mildred Humble-Smith had another great advantage which had been denied to Flora, she had been to university. She studied English at Oxford, although her degrees were conferred by Edinburgh and Durham Universities in the days when Oxford colleges still refused degrees to their women students.

When Mildred Humble-Smith's husband gave up his connection with the Brazilian navy he bought a market garden at Wimborne in Dorset. It was from the bungalow there that his wife began to submit her work to *The Catholic Fireside*; Mildred was a devout Catholic as well as an aspiring writer, so the magazine was an obvious market for her to try. She began to be mentioned in Flora's competition results in 1923 and 1924, then she began to submit stories and articles to the magazine independently.

Flora and Mildred met and became friends. The only time Mildred was away from home was when she went by train to Liphook to see Flora. The two women were soon to work together on the Postal Writers' Circle which was to occupy much of Flora's time and efforts into the next decade.

Mildred, however, was not the only friend of Flora's to contribute to her competitions, one of her own sisters had ambitions to be a writer too. Ethel Elizabeth, usually called Betty Timms, was ten years younger than Flora and also a Post Office worker. Betty won competitions in 1924 and 1925 and was to have a book published before Flora, although her talent was minimal by comparison and her work never a real success.

Flora's output doubled in the mid 1920s, in 1922 she had only written one 'Peverel Paper'[4] each month, whereas in 1923, 1924 and 1925 she produced a 'Fireside Reading Circle' article and a 'Peverel Paper' each month, an output of six to eight thousand words a month. In addition she was setting and judging the competitions and dealing with a large volume of correspondence.

Women journalists were not highly regarded in the 1920s, freelance journalists who were also wives and mothers seem to have been invisible to social commentators of the time. Flora's achievements in *The Catholic Fireside* are a tribute to her talent and ambition as well as to her capacity for hard work. Although she spent hours every day at her desk and many hours walking in search of copy for her nature articles, her home life did not suffer. She was known to be a devoted mother and brought up three children successfully; they each retained great affection for her throughout their lives.

Her nature articles in 1925 show an awareness of the need for conservation in the countryside, an awareness which was to be slow in coming to the public at large. In February 1925 she wrote about hedgerows already disappearing then (miles of English hedgerows were to disappear in the next four decades). Flora wrote of a Hampshire hedge:

> The hedgerow is so crammed with interest that it would provide studies for more hours than there are in the day. It is one of the old double hedges which, thickened with trees and twined about with creepers, used to be a common feature in English scenery. Such hedgerows used to be, and still are, where they have been retained, both gardens for every kind of wild flower and sanctuaries for birds and lesser animals.... Such hedgerows are gradually disappearing, together with the small, irregularly shaped fields they bounded. The modern scientific farmer does not approve of such waste of space and harbourage for 'vermin'. In highly farmed districts, the old, untidy, picturesque hedgerow is doomed.[5]

Footpaths were another of her interests. She had grown up in an era when footpaths were still much used by country people, but by the 1920s she could see that footpaths were under threat. In one of her 'Peverel Papers' she wrote:

> It is a pity that paths should become disused, for the footpath way is the people's immemorial right, and in the past astonishing battles have been fought to keep open some threatened one. Now they are allowed to lapse without a protest, partly, no doubt, because there is less need of them, but also because they are closed so quietly and gradually that the public does not realise what is happening.
> Years ago, if a farmer or squire wished to close a path and imagined they had the right to do so, they adopted high handed methods: fields were ploughed over the paths, gates shut and locked and barbed wire spread to punish the unwary. Then came the people in a body; gates were thrown off hinges, wire was cut,

and those who never went for a walk from one year's end to another put on their Sunday clothes and promenaded with their various progeny. Now a little is taken at a time. A ploughed up footpath turns back those with light stockings; a five barred gate with padlock and chain is substituted for an old kissing gate. Lastly and most effective of all, a house is built somewhere beside the track, the footpath carefully preserved as the law requires but reduced to the narrowest and straightest of ways fenced in with high boards or barbed wire. Very soon in such cases the old public way is abandoned to nettles and briars until such time as the law shall allow the landlord to close it officially as disused.[6]

Since Flora wrote that, miles of English footpaths have disappeared.

Flora joined an Antiquarian and Field Study Society connected with Haslemere museum at this time. One of the activities she enjoyed were walks in the autumn woods looking for fungi, which she sometimes took home to eat. When she cooked strange fungi John would not touch them, nor would he allow the children to try them. As Flora wrote many years later in a letter, 'I ate alone with the fascinated eyes of the whole family upon me, nobody quite sure whether I might not drop down dead, and that of course was too dull to keep up.'[7]

By 1925 Flora knew the area around Liphook so well that she was asked to write its guidebook. She enjoyed the project which involved her in her favourite occupations, research and writing, and revisiting local beauty spots. Her guidebook mixes history with dutiful extolling of Liphook's attractions for visitors and her own descriptions of the surrounding countryside. Writing of one of her favourite places, Weaver's Down, she said:

From the summit upon a clear day, a magnificent view rewards the climber; heath and woodland, green field and glinting stream lie stretched at his feet, a perfect panorama of beauty. Forest Mere Lake lies like a mirror in the woods directly beneath: to the south is the blue ridge of the South Downs, to the north the heathery heights of Hindhead. It does not come within the scope of this present work to dwell on the beauty and interest of this spot more fully, the present writer hopes to deal with it more fully in a future book, but the geologist, the naturalist or the nature lover will each find a happy hunting ground there, and one which has scarcely been touched upon since Gilbert White wrote of it.[8]

The future book she mentioned was never written. Although she continued to write about the Hampshire countryside for a few more years, Flora never wrote a Hampshire book; 'The Peverel Papers' remain as testimony to her great love of the county. Thirty years after her death, a selection of 'The Peverel Papers' was to appear as *A Country Calendar*,[9] chosen and edited by Margaret Lane and later still, in 1986, a larger selection was published as *The Peverel Papers*[10] edited by Julian Shuckburgh. But as far as Flora knew, the quarter of a million words she wrote about Hampshire were as ephemeral as the mayflies she observed for a June Peverel Paper: 'At last, upon some sunny morning in May or June, the final metamorphosis takes place, the shell splits, and a shining winged May Fly emerges to dance its one day in the sun, and so complete the cycle.'[11]

Once, at the very end of her life, Flora did try to put 'The Peverel Papers'[12] together as a book and her publishers were interested, but the idea came to nothing and it was left to others to complete the cycle of her nature articles by giving them the audience they deserve.

In the later 'Peverel Papers' Flora began to include more references to her childhood in Juniper Hill, presaging the work she was to do in *Lark Rise*.[13] Queenie and Old Sally appeared and the country rituals of May Day and Harvest Home were described. Flora was finding her voice.

Her knowledge of natural history was now extensive, she had studied Gilbert White, Linnaeus and Darwin and she could draw on a lifetime of her own observations. She read the rural writers of her day but she did not imitate them, her style was always recognizably a woman's work, clear and feminine. Her touch is lighter than W.H. Hudson's and less intense than those of Richard Jefferies or Edward Thomas. Lacking a classical education she could not sprinkle her work with classical references as so many male writers did; Pan and Apollo did not inhabit Peverel Woods. If Flora mentioned myth and legend, and she did so rarely, her reference points were closer to home. Merlin is mentioned sometimes, and that most British of legendary figures seems more at home in Hampshire, than a Greek or Roman would have been.

She still walked miles every week in search of material for her articles. Sometimes she was glad of a few wet days when she was forced to stay indoors. She wrote in one of her 'Peverel Papers':

'I am by nature such a truant, lured out of doors by every passing breeze or sunbeam that I have to depend on spells of really bad weather to keep me indoors for long enough together to accomplish anything.'[14]

Her children were growing up now. Winifred, or 'Diana' as everyone knew her, was working in the Post Office with her father, Basil, still a teenager was dreaming of emigrating to Australia, Peter was a lively little boy, who was sometimes looked after by a girl employed by Flora to take him for walks whilst she worked.

During the 1920s Flora had taught herself to be a photographer so that she could illustrate her articles. People who knew her in Liphook remember seeing her out on her walks carrying a box camera and taking photographs of the local scenery. It was a useful hobby for a freelance journalist and many of her 'Peverel Papers'[15] are illustrated by photographs which she took herself.

John Thompson's favourite relaxation was fishing, a hobby he probably acquired during his seaside boyhood on the Isle of Wight. With two postmen friends he often went fishing in one of the many lakes near Liphook. The land around Waggoners Wells had been given to The National Trust and had become a popular local beauty spot, with a tea garden for visitors which advertised, 'luncheons and dainty teas in the very heart of miniature Lakeland and Rustic country'. Flora must have been somewhat dismayed to realize that her own contribution to the area's popularity through the guidebook, was helping to change it from a place of wild beauty to a tourist attraction. In the Liphook guide she had written of Waggoners Wells:

These three lakes lie along the bottom of a narrow valley, acres of wild heath and woodland surround them on either side, immemorial forest trees line the banks and overhang the still green water, every leaf and twig reflected as in a mirror, so perfectly is the image embossed there that it reminds one irresistibly of the old fabulous drowned forests of legend.

Flora had been sad to find on her return to the area in 1916, that the wishing well in the woods had fallen into disuse, the custom of casting pins into the water for good luck discontinued and the well neglected. She would be pleased to see the wishing well now restored and full of coins cast in by hopeful visitors once again.

During 1925 Flora decided that she wanted to do more to help the many hopeful would-be writers who entered her competitions in *The Catholic Fireside*, so she brought 'The Fireside Reading Circle' to an end, the last competition appearing in November 1925. She then began her own postal writers group with Mildred Humble-Smith, which she called 'The Peverel Society'.

Through Dr Macfie she was able to get Lady Margaret Sackville to agree to be the society's patron, her name appearing as such on the title page of the society's booklet. Lady Margaret Sackville was the beautiful and aristocratic writer who had collaborated with Ronald Macfie in writing books of fairy tales. She was a prolific writer of verse dramas, lyrics and nature poems and she was to play a small, but significant part in Flora's life.

Margaret Sackville moved in literary circles far removed from Flora's world. At the turn of the century she had been a frequent guest at the Sussex home of the poet Wilfred Scawen Blunt where she had mixed with the literati of the day. She gave nothing but her name as patron of Flora's society but Flora was grateful for her support. It is ironic that Lady Sackville's poems are hardly remembered now when Flora's books have become classics. The most enduring memorial to Margaret Sackville is a bronze bust entitled Atlanta by Scotland's Sculptor Royal, which is in Aberdeen Art Gallery. The bronze head of Flora, which stands outside the Post Office in Liphook, is appropriately a more rugged piece of work and visited by far more literary pilgrims.

The Peverel Society was advertised in *The Catholic Fireside* with advertisements offering writing courses, conducted by 'Flora Thompson author of Bog-Myrtle and Peat and Peverel Papers and Myldrede Humble-Smith, Honours English Language and Literature, Oxon, B.Litt Durham.' Flora wrote courses on literary techniques, short story writing, verse writing and general culture. The verse writing course is as good an explanation of poetic techniques as many published between hard covers. Flora made an excellent teacher. She knew from personal experience the difficulties of being a self-taught writer, and she understood the loneliness and the need for encouragement.

Members of The Peverel Society paid an annual subscription and sent in one entry each month, a poem, a story or an article. Flora then grouped the writers into circles and a portfolio went by post from member to member until the whole circle had read and commented on each entry. A dozen portfolios circulated all over the British Isles, giving the society's members a chance to receive sympathetic criticism from other writers. Flora had the final verdict on each piece. Those who wished to do so, paid separately to receive one of the courses written by Flora, but as the society developed it became clear that members had a need for more than instruction or criticism, they needed friendship.

The Peverel Society could easily have become little more than a lonely hearts club, one of its advertisements was headed, 'There is no need to be lonely, The Peverel Society offers sympathetic criticism to literary aspirants. New friendships and new interests to all.' But Flora kept it firmly centred on literature, although the circulating portfolios did eventually also contain The Chats Book, it covered topics of literary interest and established many friendships amongst the members. Cynics could easily mock the aims of the society but Flora had real concern for the struggles of her members. A great deal of her time and creative energy went into helping her writers and it was not time wasted. According to her daughter, writing to Flora's publishers years later, 'Many of these young writers got into print and are going strong now.' Many gave up too, discouraged by their lack of success or because their families thought their work a waste of time, but Flora believed in what she was doing. If she had been one who always counted the cost to herself each time she picked up her pen, she could never have written her books. The Peverel Society may have delayed her development as a writer by taking up so much of her time, or it may have been part of a necessary stage in her maturing as a woman and a writer. At fifty Flora was not ready to write her autobiography. The flowering of genius has its own timescale.

Amongst Flora's other work at this time was the less enjoyable period she spent ghost writing for a big game hunter. Perhaps the pleasant memories she had of her old friend 'Mr Foreshaw' the retired game hunter she had known in Grayshott, prompted her to reply to an advertisement in a literary journal for a writer prepared to ghost write articles. These eventually appeared in *The Scottish Field, Chambers' Journal* and some African papers. It was writing experience of a sort, but it was in every sense foreign to her and did nothing to make her name known.

The Peverel Society flourished and Flora was still writing

'The Peverel Papers'[16] each month for *The Catholic Fireside*. Her walks in search of material for her articles took her often onto Weaver's Down. To get there she walked out of Liphook through the hamlet of Griggs Green. In the autumn of 1925 she watched the fern cutters at work there harvesting bracken:

> During the last few sunny days the bracken has got one stage nearer to carrying, having been raked into heaps, or cocks as they are called, and in a day or two, if the weather remains fine, it will be carried and built into the small circular ricks which are such a picturesque feature of the cottage gardens around the heath.

Flora was soon to find a cottage under Weaver's Down, where she could fulfil her dream of living on the heath.

12 Griggs Green

In 1926 Flora persuaded John to buy a small house which had been built in the hamlet of Griggs Green on the outskirts of Liphook. The Post Office had decided to appoint a caretaker switchboard operator to answer Liphook's night-time telephone calls, so John Thompson was relieved of his night-time telephone duties which allowed the Thompsons to consider moving house. For a short time after they moved, until the caretaker was recruited, John returned to the Post Office from Griggs Green each evening to take over the night-shift from Winifred, but soon they were able to settle down to family life in their new home.

It had long been Flora's dream to have a house of her own choosing out in the country, away from the Post Office. The house was on the long road out of Liphook which leads to Woolmer Forest. It was the perfect spot for Flora, under Weaver's Down and within reach of all the places she loved. She called the house Woolmer Cottage and although it had no mains services, was newly built and raw, she loved it.

Ownership of Woolmer Cottage carried commoners' rights, so Flora could gather wood for her fire 'by hook or by crook,' taking to burn any dead or fallen wood providing that she did not, 'take axe or billock to lop stick or stock'. It is a curious irony that someone who was to write so cloquently about the dispossessed commoners of Juniper Hill should, in the 1920s live in a house with commoners' rights, even though those rights were only an echo of what had once been a way of life.

At Woolmer Cottage there was no busy pavement under her windows, no chance that she could be called into the office to help at the counter. The house was backed by pine trees and surrounded by sandy tracks leading to the downs and woods. Flora was at peace there. When her family left the house after breakfast and the chores were done, she could write when it rained, with only the wind in the trees for company and when the days were fine her favourite walks were on her doorstep. On some of her afternoon walks she was accompanied by her daughter, who worked split shifts at the Post Office telephone exchange, from 9 a.m.–1 p.m. and 4.30 p.m.–8 p.m., which left her free to spend the afternoons with her mother. Some who knew them remember them being more like sisters than mother and daughter.

Flora's only worry at this time was concern for her eldest son Basil who had set off for Australia with another young man from Liphook who was engaged to Winifred. The journey to Australia was long and not without its dangers, but Flora and John did have the comfort of knowing that their son was going out to stay with his uncle, Flora's brother Frank, in Queensland to begin with. Winifred too was concerned about the departure of her brother and her fiancé; her engagement was not to survive the parting.

The Thompsons' neighbours at Griggs Green were the Leggett family who lived at Grove House. Mr Leggett ran a small farm on Weaver's Down. His son Joe was the boy who had so often met Flora out walking years before and had been persuaded by her to give up bird nesting. By the time the Thompsons moved in next door, Joe was no longer enjoying the freedom of the fields but was hard at work on his father's farm. It was he who first made contact with the new neighbours. One day he noticed Peter staring longingly over the dividing fence as he hitched the farm mule to a cart. The little boy asked where he was going and if he could go too, Joe Leggett suggested that he asked his mother. Mr Leggett recalls:

> As I left for Weaver's Down Peter and his mother were at their gate and he was trusted into my care with instructions to show him all the interesting things to be seen on the farm. Then,

thanking me for taking him, Mrs Thompson remarked, 'it allows me time to work in my study without being disturbed.' I wondered, but did not ask, what sort of work she was doing in her study, painting I imagined. It became a regular thing for Peter to come to the farm with me and regular too for his mother to thank me and brief me before leaving.[1]

Joe Leggett was not the only person who was puzzled to know what Mrs Thompson did. She remained a mystery to local people who had always thought her wandering about the countryside very odd. They were curious too about her habit of inviting gipsies into her home. Flora had always had a great love of gipsies and stories about them occur frequently in her work. Local people were baffled by her interest in such social outcasts.

Flora's love of gipsies was fired by her own romantic dreams of a life of complete freedom in the countryside, in one sense she too was a traveller. She knew that their lives were hard and that they were often dishonest but she remained fascinated by them. In one of her 'Peverel Papers' she wrote of the gipsy girl who visited her with her brothers and sisters bringing: 'A small offering, a rare orchid from the bog, or a chipped flint which they think may be a stone arrow head, such as they know I search for and cherish. Or they will plait me a tiny rush basket and fill it with a fern to hang in my window.'[2]

Flora kept her contacts with most local people down to friendly comments about the weather or the seasons, gossip was her pet aversion and she kept herself aloof from it. Only once did she ask for information about a local scandal. Joe Leggett recalls her asking him about a smallholder who was caught stealing pig food from his father's farm to fatten his own pigs, the culprit was a lay-reader in the chapel. Mr Leggett remembers: 'She was horrified to think that a man could do such a thing and asked me for accurate details of the incident. She never made notes but I felt that all I said was registering.'[3]

Years later that particular incident appeared in *Candleford Green*[4] cleverly disguised as if it had happened in Oxfordshire. Flora's habit of harvesting stories from one county and setting them in another, makes her books belong, not to any particular place but simply to rural England.

It is not surprising that people felt that there was something unusual in the reserve of this quiet woman, who said so little and observed all. She understood people far better than they

understood her. She was an enigma; they were as readable as
books to her perceptive mind.

When buying eggs one day at a cottage she commented to the
occupant that the celandines at her gate were cheerful:

> 'Oh them', she said vaguely, when in answer to her uncompre-
> hending look I pointed to a whole flood of living sunshine upon
> the bank by her gateway, 'don't know as I've ever noticed 'em
> before.'

Flora concealed her astonishment, understanding well that
country people hate to appear behindhand with strangers in
nature knowledge.

Eileen Leggett, Joe's sister from Grove House, remembers
Flora well from this period. She writes:

> We knew nothing about her being a writer but my mother, a keen
> judge of character, soon decided that Mrs Thompson was a
> 'lady' but her husband no 'gentleman'. People think she was
> intimidated by him but (at least by the time I knew them) in her
> gentle way she managed him nicely.[5]

Eileen Leggett had always worked on her father's farm but
Flora encouraged her to apply for a job as part-time operator at
the Liphook telephone exchange and persuaded John to support
her application. So started two years or more of Eileen's
friendship with Winifred, with whom she worked at the Post
Office, and with Flora. She remembers John Thompson as very
aloof and not popular with the postal staff: fair but very strict.

The Leggetts found Flora Thompson a delightful neighbour,
unobtrusive and uncomplaining about their noisy farming
activities. Eileen took to visiting her every Thursday afternoon
for a chat, and a listen to the Thompson's wireless, though she
always left at four o'clock so that Flora could listen to Choral
Evensong which she loved.

A frequent visitor to Liphook at this time was Flora's sister
Betty who shared her interest in writing. During 1926 Betty had
a book of children's stories accepted for publication. The book
was called *The Little Grey Men of the Moor*.[6] The stories about
gnomes on Dartmoor, are slight and stiff but Flora was proud of
her sister's achievement. Apart from Edwin who had been dead
for ten years, Betty was the only member of Flora's family to
share her literary interests.

Mildred Humble-Smith also had a children's book published,

it was a book of school stories in the Angela Brazil mould called *Girls of Chiltern Towers*.[7] Flora's ambition to publish a full-length book was not to be achieved for another decade. She was still struggling to find the right way to use all the material and memories which she had been storing since her childhood.

'Peverel Papers'[8] continued to give her an outlet for her observations of nature. Everywhere she walked she saw something that she wanted to share with others. Although she was a solitary by nature, Flora felt that she had a responsibility to share the sights and insights granted to her.

Margaret Lane in her biographical essay on Flora[9] claimed that her life had afforded her little satisfaction and yet over and over again in 'Peverel Papers'[10] Flora wrote of her pleasures. She described being up at dawn to pick mushrooms, records her adventures by train and on foot into Sussex and on the South Downs. At this middle period of her life Flora had almost complete freedom to do what she enjoyed, to write about it and to sell her work. One July day she wrote: 'I set out with my Thermos and sandwiches for a day in the open. I did well to start early, for the sun, already high in a cloudless sky, gave promise of great heat.'[11] On that perfect day she met her friends the gipsy children picking whortleberries and she was struck by the beauty of the Guelder Rose and a dozen other details of the summer countryside. This open-air freedom and an outlet for her creative response to it, gave Flora a very generous measure of satisfaction which she often acknowledged in print.

During 1926 and 1927 Flora continued to write one 'Peverel Paper'[12] each month. Only in May 1926 did an article fail to appear, when the General Strike prevented the magazine from publishing. Such was the popularity of the articles that two were printed the following month. The Peverel Society was growing and she was busy compiling a book of verse by society members. The first *Peverel Society Book of Verse*[13] was advertised in *The Catholic Fireside* in August 1926. The book was well produced and Flora was able to get it reviewed in very reputable journals including *The Times Literary Supplement*. It is a tribute to the members' verses and to Flora's compilation of the anthology, that such a prestigious paper should review the book. The review reads:

Poetry is a means of communion as well as of personal

expression and such fellowships as the Peverel Society who draw their members from all parts of the British Isles and link them together by monthly circulating portfolios of verse, satisfy a real need, even if none of this verse appeared in print. Lovers, however, of graceful, unpretentious verse outside the fellowship will appreciate this little anthology, which contains many poems which have a quiet distinction, and none which are insincere.[14]

But by the time that review was published Flora was no longer living in Hampshire. In 1927 John Thompson saw an advertisement in the *Post Office Circular* for the job of Postmaster in Dartmouth, Devon. He applied for the job and was appointed in August 1927. Flora was appalled. She found it hard to forgive her husband for uprooting the family so recently settled and so happy in their new home. John was fifty-three, he had only seven more years to work before compulsory retirement from the Post Office. It was the achievement of all his ambitions to be Postmaster of a sizeable town and, whatever her feelings, Flora was expected to be a dutiful wife and follow him.

It has been claimed that John, unlike Flora, was not a true countryman and therefore did not enjoy life in rural Hampshire, but perhaps it is fairer to say that he was missing the sea. He had had a seaside childhood on the Isle of Wight and as a young man had chosen to work in Bournemouth, his father was a naval man so the sea was in John's blood. Both of his sons were eventually to go to sea, so Dartmouth had much to recommend it. Flora had not enjoyed Bournemouth, hers was an inland spirit bound to the earth by woods and fields. But wives in the 1920s went where their breadwinner went.

Before John left Liphook for Dartmouth, one Thursday afternoon, he was presented with a cheque for £40. A small committee of local gentry had organized the collection of this testimonial to John Thompson's service in Liphook. The presentation was made by Captain B.D. Byfield at his home Hewshott House, a list of subscribers accompanying the cheque. The report of the presentation in the local paper said that John Thompson was ' ... courteous, obliging and willing to help whenever possible.' Forty pounds was a considerable sum in 1927 and must show that he was held in high regard by some of his customers. If his staff did find him rather too strict, John Thompson obviously ran an efficient Post Office and telephone exchange and gave a service which was much appreciated locally.

In December of 1927 Flora's last 'Peverel Paper'[15] appeared. In it she wrote of winter birds, hedge cutting and the gipsies who wintered on the heath. She did not tell her faithful readers that her series of nature articles was at an end. Being a December feature the last 'Peverel Paper' has a distinctly Christmas feel about it:

> ... faraway stirrings of a more crowded life invade the quiet of the country. The postman comes oftener and more heavily laden; parcel vans from the big London stores flash along country lanes: railway trucks at village stations are piled with berried holly for the London market, and long after twilight has fallen upon dark heath and glinting water, a bright humid glow upon the horizon marks the whereabouts of the nearest town ... but apart from that there is something very restful about these short grey days before Christmas. Now, if ever, nature seems to stand still for a space. The trees are leafless, the pools stilled under their thin ice crust, the heath is darkly sleeping, and the fields bare under the grey sky.[16]

The *Catholic Fireside* readers who enjoyed the 'Peverel Papers' must have been disappointed to find no more of Flora's articles in the magazine's New Year issues.

Whilst John settled into his new job in Devon and looked for a house for his family, Flora, Winifred and Peter remained in Hampshire. For a long time John was unable to find a suitable house to buy in Dartmouth and until he did, Woolmer Cottage was not put on the market so Flora remained in Hampshire for almost another year. It is easy to imagine the poignant pleasures of that year, when Flora had so much time to herself and the Hampshire countryside became the more dear because she was so soon to leave it.

Eileen Leggett recalls Flora roaming around her father's farm, taking a great interest in some derelict cottages. She was fascinated by the lives of those who had last lived in the cottages and asked about them when she called at the farm for butter, milk, or fruit for her jam making.

One which she wrote about, had roses and honeysuckle on the moss-grown roof and pretty diamond-paned windows but when Flora looked inside, she found rooms no larger than ships' cabins and a windowless hole which had served as a larder. She guessed that ten or more children had been born and brought up in the tiny rooms and bodies awaited burial there.

> A little thought given to this aspect of the good old times ... should help to reconcile us to the red brick boxes of dwellings which at other times have seemed a blot upon the countryside. They have at least weatherproof roofs and serviceable sash windows. The ugliness, let us hope, is but a passing phase. As people read more and think more, taste must follow. Future generations will demand beauty as well as usefulness. This is but a time of transition.[17]

Many would say now, that that period of transition lasted for another half century.

In the spring of 1928 Flora filled the garden of her home with flowers, although she claimed not to be a very patient or a very skilled gardener, she enjoyed creating the masses of colour which her neighbours were to remember at Woolmer Cottage: dahlias; amber, orange and gold nasturtiums and marigolds made a defiant blaze in the cottage garden that last summer.

Finally a house was found in Dartmouth, Woolmer Cottage was sold and the move to Devon was arranged for the autumn. Basil Thompson came home from Australia with the news that Winifred's fiancé wanted to end their engagement, autumn 1928 was an unhappy time for Flora and her daughter.

The move was traumatic. John came back from Dartmouth to help his wife and Basil was sent ahead to Devon to prepare for their arrival in the house which John had bought, but the weather could not be organized and on the day of the move it rained ceaselessly. Flora left a record of the move in a fragment of unpublished work:

> On the day of our journey, rain poured down from morning to night without ceasing. My last glimpse of the snug little red-tiled cottage with a backing of pine trees which had been our home was one of desolation. Trees dripped heavily, the lawn before the house was a swamp and the flowers left in the borders were drooping and draggled. Indoors the removal men were in possession and before I was in the taxi which was to take us to the station, packages carefully chalked PLEASE KEEP DRY were standing outside the front door on the gravel. But there was not time to go back, even my momentary pause beside the grave of a

faithful old dog produced a chorus of expostulation from the assembled and waiting family.[18]

The wrench was made, her roots were being torn up, like those of another rural writer Mary Russell Mitford, who wrote when forced to move from a beloved home, 'What a tearing up by the roots it was, I have pitied cabbage plants, celery and all transplantable things ever since.'[19]

Crammed into the taxi which finally pulled away from Woolmer Cottage were John and Flora, Winifred and Peter, sundry suitcases and bundles and Flora's portable typewriter which she thought too precious to trust to the removal men.

The family travelled by train, out of Hampshire, through Dorset, into Devon, the countryside for the whole journey recorded by Flora as 'a moving wet blurr of green'. Perhaps she thought as she travelled, of the birds she had written about in an autumn 'Peverel Paper':

When their recognised signs of winter appear, the native birds near the coast go with the first favourable wind; and presently other birds from further north take their places to await their turn, and so on, until all have gone excepting a few stragglers who make their way to Devonshire and Cornwall for the winter.[20]

Peter passed his time clearing spy holes in the glass to observe level crossings, signal boxes and gangs of plate layers. He had with him a back number of *The Engineer* lent to him by Basil who had decided to abandon sheep farming in favour of an engineering career. Peter was eager to see the sea and restless on the long journey. Winifred, still known to all as Diana, seemed aloof from it all, she was not sorry to be leaving Liphook and her broken engagement behind. Flora observed her fellow passengers to divert her mind and John dozed behind his newspaper, except at stations where he helped women travellers with their suitcases or market baskets.

Devon was unknown territory to Flora, it had no associations for her, personal or literary but it was to be the setting for the final flowering of her genius. Had she been able to remain in Hampshire or even to return to her Oxfordshire roots, she might never have felt driven to record her inland childhood as she did exiled in Devon.

13   Back to the Beginning

As the train carrying the Thompson family approached Dartmouth, Peter became increasingly excited. The train emerged from Greenway tunnel and began to run beside the river where Peter could see some of the shipping laid up in the river. Dartmouth, like most ports in the inter-war years, was caught in a slump. There was a world surplus of shipping but to a ten-year-old boy like Peter, who was enthralled by ships and engines, the sight of masts and funnels meant excitement not economic gloom. The old railway bridge across Noss Creek had just been abandoned as unsafe, so the train took the new diversion around the creek, where Phillips' shipyard specialized in building lightships for Trinity House. Dartmouth had two shipyards, one each side of the river, both under the same ownership by the 1920s. In the 1930s, when he left school, Peter was to become an engineering apprentice at Phillips' shipyard. His first sight of the shipyards on the river, seen from the train, made a lasting impression on him.

John had rediscovered his love for the sea since he started work in Dartmouth. His father had been in the navy in the early days of steam and John was brought up in sight of the Solent. His father's skills missed a generation and appeared in his grandsons, Basil and Peter, who both became marine engineers.

The Thompson family arrived at Kingswear Station on that wet day in 1928 at the end of their journey from Hampshire. The station is dramatically sited at the edge of the Dart estuary with the town of Dartmouth spread out on the hills across the river. When Flora stood on the platform she had her first glimpse of the town which was to be her new home.

From the station the family had to cross the river by ferry. As the ferry boat took them nearer to the Dartmouth shore, John pointed out their new house, The Outlook, to those members of the family who had not seen it before. Even on a damp day the house is easy to pick out from the houses set high on the hill above the River Dart. The Post Office too was easy to pick out in its position on the waterfront. No one knows if Flora had ever seen her new home before, possibly she left the choosing entirely to John, having had little heart for house hunting herself.

The house to which they were travelling, The Outlook, is in the area called Above Town, a road cut into the hills above the river at the southern end of the town. The house is reached by a very steep road which leads up from the town centre. Flora was later to discover the pretty alley-ways with their steep steps and high walls, which run up from South Town to Above Town. There are no streets higher than Above Town even today, the terrain is so steep and wooded, it was some consolation to Flora to find that her new home was backed by open fields and woods. The house itself is one of a pair of substantial gabled houses not unlike the Thompsons' Bournemouth home, only its splendid situation saves it from being suburban. As the house is approached by a set of very steep steps, the removal men had quite a task to get the Thompsons' furniture up to it when the van arrived from Hampshire.

When Flora went into her new home she found the views from the square bay windows of the house breathtaking. Opposite, across the river, are the wooded hills and scattered houses of Kingswear, to the left the roofs of Dartmouth but most spectacular of all, is the view down river, where the Dart spreads between thickly wooded hills towards the open sea.

In the spring of 1929 Flora began to explore her surroundings as the days grew warmer and longer, and the Devonshire scenery was at its best. Behind her house, beyond a thin spinney, is the steep open ground of Dyers Hill, to the south the hill is thickly wooded and in the spring Flora found these woods full of primroses, violets, wood anemones and bluebells. On one of her walks in June she was to count thirty-two varieties of wild flower on Jawbone Hill behind Above Town.

John took her to Dartmoor which she loved and when she began to write again, she wrote poems about Dartmoor, the Tors, the heather slopes, the streams and Wisemans Wood. It was the sort of unspoiled, wild landscape that she loved. It was not Hampshire but she found Devon beautiful.

Flora went for a short walk soon after her arrival in Dartmouth, round Warfleet Creek to St Petrox Church and Castle Cove. St Petrox is a tiny medieval church built beside the castle, which guards the harbour entrance. It had not been in regular use since the nineteenth century but services were, and still are, held there in the summer months. When Flora knew it the church had some new memorials, the west window had been unblocked as a memorial to the men of the parish who died in the great war and in 1927 a central east window had been installed in memory of a celebrated engineer, something which Flora may have shown to Peter who wanted to be an engineer himself. Flora could not, in her wildest nightmares, have dreamed how soon Peter's name was to be recorded in the little church.

Flora wrote of a Sunday walk she made, out to the point where the sea and the estuary meet, in a fragment of unpublished verse:

> Here where the sea-spume meets the land mist
> And rocks and glistening trails of seaweed fringe the bank
> Of shell-white violets and fern and moss and seabirds scream
> to warn away the human
> One who has ventured hither this wet Sunday morning
> Only one trail of footprints on the shingle
> To witness to the town of seven thousand
> Where parsons preach and housewives cook and men lay late
> abed,
> In honour of the Sabbath, while the rain
> Slants o'er the hills and pelts into the sea.[1]

A few years earlier Flora had written in a 'Peverel Paper', an account of a walk she took on a beach beneath Hengistbury Head on the Solent. She wrote:

The tide was receding. The sandstone rocks beneath the head were dark and dripping; the pools were full of stranded things left by the sea. The one nearest to me was a world in miniature. Many living things strange to me and beyond my knowledge hid in the crevices of rocks, or swayed gently in the water. Some day, if ever I live near the sea again, I hope to learn more of them, but yesterday I poked amongst them with the ignorant pleasure of a child.[2]

Castle Point at Dartmouth and all the coves beyond the harbour mouth, were to give Flora hours of delight as she explored rock pools, learning more on each of her walks, of the life of the shoreline. In the town's old bookshops she searched dusty shelves for books on marine life, always eager to learn; every new aspect of the natural world held enchantment for Flora.

John had made himself at home in Dartmouth very quickly. He was already settled in his job when the family joined him and before long he acquired a boat called *Sea Mew* which he kept at Lidstone's boatyard, a short walk from Above Town. John and Peter spent every spare minute at the boatyard or out on the water, leaving Flora to explore her new surroundings. John was to be remembered in the town as a dapper man fond of taking his small boat too far out to sea.

John went out fishing with Dr Max Tylor, a local GP whose second wife Christine soon became Flora's friend. Christine Tylor was a great admirer of Jane Austen's work and the two women discovered that they shared a love of books.

Dr Tylor's son Richard, who was the first County Branch Librarian in Dartmouth remembers meeting Flora. She made a vivid impression on him as she was so unlike the usual run of borrowers who came to the library. She told him that she had written a nature column in a national magazine for eight years. Although it was to be some time before Flora's work became well known, the Tylor family knew her as a writer in the 1930s and she was not the recluse that some have supposed her to have been in Devon at that time.

Dr Tylor's house was in Newcomen Road below Above Town; to call on Christine Tylor, Flora had only to walk down one of the three sets of steps which joined the two roads. She could choose from St Petrox Steps narrow damp and ancient, Nelson Steps which turn and twist between tall houses, or

Chapel Steps, a wider set of steps between walls which are decorated with wallflowers, red valerian, navelwort and mosses in their season. Although Flora missed Weaver's Down and Woolmer Forest she was quick to appreciate the beauties of Dartmouth.

Peter was just the right age to enjoy the town which was a boy's paradise. The harbour was visited by all sorts of craft, from passenger ships, to cargo ships and the fishing fleet. There was an annual regatta for a week each summer, when the town was thronged with sailing people and the harbour full of yachts. There were rowing and swimming races, even the local trawlers put on a race. Peter and his father enjoyed it all immensely. In their small boat *Sea Mew* they sailed around the river in the evening to look at the yachts in their regatta rig. In years to come Peter was to crew on a yacht chartered by the editor of *Punch*, after *Punch* had featured a review of Flora's books.

Flora's long association with *The Catholic Fireside* magazine had ended when she left Hampshire. When she no longer had her monthly nature articles to write, she returned to writing short stories for a time, trying out stories with Devon backgrounds. Two which remain amongst her papers are set in the sea-port of 'Britmouth'. One tells the story of the last days of an old sailor, the other is the story of a lonely woman who lives in a solitary cottage above Compass Cove. There is still a solitary cottage above Compass Cove in- Dartmouth. The stories are well constructed, as could be expected of a writer who taught short story writing, but they do not quite succeed and seem never to have appeared in print.[3]

Middle-aged women appear in many of Flora's stories at this time, she was herself in her early fifties and, like her heroines, experiencing the pleasures of more free time. In two of her stories middle-aged women plan to use talents previously sacrificed to domestic demands, one wants to write, the other to paint. Each is denied the opportunity in the dénouement of the story. It was a situation with which Flora identified closely, she longed to achieve her literary ambitions. The Peverel Society took up much of her time, her faithful members still writing to express their gratitude for her encouragement. The annual subscription was now seven and sixpence payable to The Secretary, The Peverel Society, Dartmouth.

Flora still wanted to be a poet, encouraged in her hope by

Ronald Macfie with whom she continued to correspond. In one of her earlier comments to a Peverel Society member who sent poems for her criticism she wrote: 'I am afraid I cannot encourage you to hope for success in poetry. Yours is the particular blend of commonsense touched with humour which is best expressed in prose.'

How close that comes to a summary of her own talent. Perhaps she would have taken her own advice to write prose, if she had in her reading, come across a remark of Mary Russell Mitford's in a letter, 'You are aware, I hope, that all clever people begin by writing bad poetry.'[4]

Flora's was not bad poetry, it was good verse, but no more, an example of her verse is:

The Earthly Paradise

When I am old
Give me for heaven a little house set on a heath:
The blue hills behind; the blue sea before.
The brick floor scoured crimson, the flagstones like snow;
The brass taps and candlesticks like gold,
And there, in my soft grey gown between the hollyhocks,
Upon a day of days I would welcome an old poet;
And pour him tea, and walk upon the heath, and talk the sun
down;
And then by the wood fire he would read me the poems of his
passionate youth,
And make new ones praising friendship above love.[5]

That day of days never came. In 1931 Ronald Campbell Macfie died suddenly in a London nursing home, he was sixty-six. When Flora heard the news of his death she wrote his name on the fly leaf of a book adding a quotation from Shakespeare's Cleopatra, 'The bright day is done and we are for the dark.'

She also wrote a poem sometime later when she had read one of Dr Macfie's books published after his death. His book was called *The Faiths and Heresies of a Poet Scientist.*[6] Flora's poem was called:

On Reading a Posthumous Book

Our poet's singing lips are dumb;
His body, like a noble tree,
Has fallen irrevocably;
His healing hands so quick to aid,
Are dust, and in the dust are laid.

Death hath the victory? no for here
The grave is rent, the man stands clear.
This his last gift, to us has brought
The pain pressed vintage of his thought
His life of song, his life of pain,
And, being dead, he speaks again.[7]

Another book published posthumously was Dr Macfie's *Book of Odes*[8] which was inscribed: 'That these odes should be collected and published in a companion volume to *Last Poems* and dedicated to Rose, is according to the last wish of Ronald Campbell Macfie.'

Rose was Rose Mildred Sleeman, a lady Dr Macfie had known as long as he had known Flora. In 1919 he had made a will in which he left everything to Rose and made her his literary executor. She was described in the deposition to his will as 'an intimate friend'. After his death Rose Sleeman had to dispose of all the effects of his London home, for which an inventory was prepared. Dr Macfie owned very little, his entire estate, some in Scotland and some in England, amounted to only £244.

Somewhere amongst his papers were Flora's letters, which he had kept. The fate of these letters is a mystery. When Margaret Lane was researching her essay[9] on Flora's life, she wrote to Lady Margaret Sackville to enquire about the letters, under the impression that Margaret Sackville was Dr Macfie's executor. Margaret Sackville replied that she had destroyed the letters having seen 'no point in keeping such rubbish'. Margaret Lane surmised that Lady Sackville resented Ronald Macfie's friendship with Flora, but there must have been more than resentment behind her disposal of letters, belonging to an estate of which she was not even the executor. Such an act suggests the stronger motive of jealousy. Whatever happened to the letters, their loss is a sad one, as Margaret Lane said in her essay,[10] 'there was no one else to whom Flora had been able to write so freely about her life, her work and her hopes'.

In 1932 Flora heard from her sister May, who had married a Catholic, and had become a Catholic herself. Flora wrote that she hoped her sister would:

> ... find rest of soul and peace of mind in your faith. I myself stand just where I always did in that respect. I have always had a great love for the Catholic religion from a child and during the eight years I was writing for *The Catholic Fireside* I found many Catholic friends amongst my readers, including several nuns. I am fairly well instructed in the faith, as I have read many books on it, and of course have attended many services at different times, but I do not suppose I shall ever take the great step you have taken as there are family and other obstacles.[11]

Flora was never to take the great step, she remained an Anglican to her death.

In 1933 Emma Timms died at Hethe in Oxfordshire where she had been living with one of Flora's sisters after she had had to give up her home in Juniper Hill. She was eighty and had been a widow for fifteen years, living alone for much of that time in the end house, the cottage which she and Albert Timms had intended to leave fifty years before. As Flora's direct links with the past were broken, one by one, she drew nearer to starting her most important work, work which grew out of her need to capture the vanished world of her childhood.

But before she began her major work, Flora tried hard to become a novelist. Her first attempt was a long novel called *Gates of Eden*,[12] into which she wove many of the elements which were eventually to become part of her classic books. *Gates of Eden* is the romantic story of a young girl who runs away from home and falls in love. All the elements of Flora's Bournemouth meeting with Dr Macfie are in it, the heroine is a stonemason's daughter, the hero a doctor poet who is married.

In real life it was Flora, not Dr Macfie who was married and probably only she who had such romantic dreams. There were many beautiful and talented women in Ronald Macfie's life. Self-regarding romanticism is no basis for a good book and Flora was not a novelist, the book was a failure. But the typescript which remains amongst her papers, does give many hints of the material which Flora was struggling to use, parts of the book are startlingly like *Lark Rise*[13] as when the heroine,

Berengaria, or Berry for short, visits a friend whose mother
made lace:

> Berry would sit and watch the bobbins flying and listen to the
> tales, while the kettle sang on the hob and the old black cat made
> its toilet upon the red and black rag rug before the fireplace and
> the sunbeams struck down through the window and filled the
> bare room with dancing motes. The mother's stories were all of
> the past, she had a wonderful memory. Those were the old
> lacemaking days, when every woman and child sat close at their
> pillows from morning to night, and every village, every cottage
> almost, had its own jealously guarded patterns and craft secrets.
> In those days they carried their delicate merchandise to the
> Tandry Fair at the county town on Michaelmas and brought
> back money enough to pay the year's rent and provide the winter
> firing. That was a day to be sure. Booths all down the High
> Street and round the Market Place, peep shows and fat ladies,
> and tight rope dancers, tents where they took your likeness on
> glass and painted you in a gold watch and chain, whether you
> wore one or not, gingerbread stall with gilded castles and pigs
> and true lovers' knots and bars of white and pink rock as long as
> walking sticks, other stalls with lilac print dress lengths, shoes
> and whitey-brown sheets and underwear. She could see it and
> smell it all now, and even then it was nothing to what it had been
> in her grandmother's time. But what she liked best as a child,
> was the tripe supper. The boys and men, who had stayed at
> home, had everything ready and the tripe went on to heat up and
> the hot elderberry wine was sweetened and spiced and everybody
> went to bed with a full stomach and a little in their purses that
> one night in the year. 'All over and done with,' she would sigh.
> The machine lace came in when she was 12 years of age and
> ruined the handmade lace trade. Cheap as dirt the machine lace
> was and as nasty as dirt she thought it, though most people liked
> it because it was so wide and patterny. Some had even stripped
> the real old stuff off their christening robes and petticoats and
> put on the machine lace to be in fashion. The lace pillow would
> be exhibited with its band of pricked parchment, upon which the
> delicate pattern formed, while the bobbins were flung, every
> bobbin weighted with a cluster of beads, each of the clusters
> having its own history.[14]

Flora failed to handle the difficulties of construction required
to bring a long novel to a successful conclusion and her
characters lack depth, but in the writing of details like
lacemaking, she was unconsciously practising for her real work,

the writing of her life as she remembered it in the 1880s in rural Oxfordshire. The lacemaking story from *Gates of Eden* was to reappear as Queenie's story in *Lark Rise*.[15]

Flora was discerning enough to realize when she had finished *Gates of Eden*,[16] that the over-romantic story was not good, despite the months of work she had put into it. She never sent the typescript to a publisher.

In 1935 John Thompson retired from the Post Office. He had long accepted Flora's need to write and had even built a writing room for her in the steeply sloping garden of their home. In her private office Flora kept all the Peverel Society material, lists of members and their addresses, the portfolios ready to go out, or those in for her final judgement, and there she continued to experiment with poems, historical articles and with other novels started but never finished.

By the mid 1930s she had experimented with almost every kind of writing. She was nearly sixty and despite considerable success as a freelance journalist, she knew that she was not a poet or a historian, not a short story writer or a novelist: she could write nature articles and literary features, and run a postal writers' circle, but that was small beer for a woman with real literary ambitions.

14   Lark Rise

Flora sat at her desk one day in 1935 trying to find new ways of
using the material her readers had enjoyed in 'Peverel Papers':[1]
her sketches of country life and characters remembered from
her childhood. She reached for an empty diary and in the day
spaces she began to write down the verses of children's singing
games which came back to her. As she wrote, she saw in her
memory the girls gathered on summer evenings in the 1880s on
one of the green spaces between the cottages of Juniper Hill. In
the light of summer sunsets the hamlet girls had played the
singing games handed down through generations of country
children.

In Dartmouth fifty years later, Flora wrote their verses in her
diary, ready to use them when she found the right medium with
which to paint her word pictures of the past. In collecting the
children's games and rhymes, Flora pre-dated the work Iona
and Peter Opie were to do in that same field by twenty-five
years. Folk songs were already being collected, but children's
games and songs had yet to be taken seriously. In her quiet way
Flora was passionate about the past, especially the unrecorded
past life of the poor, hers was not the collector's urge but an
imaginative desire to preserve and share the country life which
she knew so well.

At her desk Flora wrote down the scraps of verse and song which came back to her – 'Waly, waly, wallflower growing up so high, we are all maidens so we must die', is scribbled in the space for Monday 21 January 1935.[2] Where household notes or appointments might have been written, Flora wrote of Lucy Ashton the youngest maid in the game she was remembering. Then she thought of the songs that the men sang at the Juniper Hill inn, the Fox; songs that the children had heard through the open bar windows on warm evenings and she jotted them down too. Although she was nearly sixty Flora had not forgotten anything that she had seen and heard as a child, she knew what acute observers children could be and she felt that they should be encouraged to look at local history, as well as national history at school. In one of her 'Peverel Papers' she had written: 'I wonder that no educationalist has suggested that the school children of a parish should be appointed its historians. It would make most interesting reading for the people of the year 2,000, this new Doomsday Book.'[3] Sixty years after Flora wrote that comment such a project was carried out by school children. In so many matters Flora was ahead of her time.

Flora and John's children were independent by this time, Basil was an engineer on ships which sailed between North and South America. Winifred had given up Post Office work and trained to be a nurse. Like her grandmother, Winifred proved to be a born nurse, Emma Timms' ambitions for Flora being fulfilled in the next generation. Peter was beginning his apprenticeship as a ship's engineer at Phillips' shipyard. In Germany the navy was being rebuilt and Hitler was gaining power.

After ten years of life in the West Country Flora had learned to love Devon, she was still active enough to enjoy long walks on the cliffs close to her home. A solitary walker, she avoided Dartmouth in the summer season when the brittle gaiety of the thirties arrived with the yachting set, their lives in acute contrast to those of the poor. Even Dartmouth had its slums in the 1930s. Flora was no longer poor herself but she did not forget what a struggle life was when lived too near the bone.

In 1936 Flora decided to send one of her short stories to *The Lady* magazine. The story called 'The Tail-less Fox' had been written in Liphook years before, for some reason Flora dug it out and submitted it. It was a story set in a cottage, not a pretty, genteel cottage, but a poor one. The heroine is a hard-working mother who has just given birth to her sixth child. It was a down-to-earth story which is perhaps why it was never published in the 1920s when it was written. In the 1930s it was a small revelation to Flora to discover that there was a market for stories of poverty, the commonplace poverty of women like the newly delivered mother whose 'hands were still sodden and corrugated from her morning at the washtub, yet strangely weak and trembling from all that had happened since'.

When *The Lady* published her story in December 1936[4] and Flora realized that if readers would read about the rural poor, she could write about her childhood in Juniper Hill, she sent another typescript to *The Lady*, this time it was not a story but an essay which appeared in April 1937 entitled 'Old Queenie'.[5] The essay about Queenie the lacemaker had all the *Lark Rise*[6] enchantments in it. Queenie sits on a low stool in her garden, with a lace pillow on her lap, delphiniums and foxgloves make a background for her lilac-print apron and sunbonnet: before her is a long bench of beehives, straw skeps with red pan roofs. With a few alterations Flora was soon to write this into the book which she had already conceived.

Flora posted another essay to a magazine called *The National Review*, an essay which she called 'An Oxfordshire Hamlet in the Eighties'.[7] The essay was a description of Juniper Hill from which only the larks were missing in the text and the title, otherwise it was substantially the first chapter of *Lark Rise*.[8] Flora had served her long apprenticeship to the craft of writing, when the essay appeared in August 1937 she was already writing a small masterpiece.

That same month Flora's eldest son Basil was married in America, he promised to bring his bride Dora home in the spring to meet his parents. Basil was an engineer with the Prince Line on the New York to Buenos Aires run so his parents saw him rarely. Flora was full of happy anticipation at the end of 1937. She wrote another essay during the winter and sent it to *The National Review* for a spring issue, it was called 'May Day in the Eighties'.[9]

Basil came home to Dartmouth with his new wife Dora early in 1938. Devon was at its best in spring and Flora was happy, she had not seen her eldest son for a long time and her work was going well. Her daughter-in-law was to remember that during their visit John actively encouraged Flora to write. He was beginning to be proud of her.

When 'May Day in the Eighties' appeared in May 1938 it opened with a paragraph about court ladies going a-maying, the last echoes of Flora's romanticism. Within months Flora had rewritten that opening paragraph in the down-to-earth style which she adopted for *Lark Rise*.[10] The chapter, still called 'May Day' in the book began:

> After the excitement of the concert came the long winter months when snowstorms left patches on the ploughed fields, like scrapings of sauce on leftover pieces of Christmas pudding, until the rains came and washed them away and the children, carrying old umbrellas to school, had them turned inside out by the wind, and cottage chimneys smoked and washing had to be dried indoors. But at last came spring and spring brought May Day, the greatest day of the year from the children's point of view.

As soon as she began to write simply of things she had seen and known. Flora produced a clear-eyed picture of a vanished world, commonplace and yet full of enchantment. She was sixty but she could recall the springtimes of her childhood with perfect clarity although she would cheerfully admit that she could not remember recent events a quarter as well as she remembered going to school for the first time, in what she called, her impressible years.

Her magazine articles on Juniper Hill had had no narrator, for *Lark Rise*[11] she found the perfect voice to bring the story to her readers, she found Laura. Laura had all the country virtues of vitality, courage and humour, which Flora conveyed with her own gifts of observation and poetic imagination.

When Flora took up her pen to begin *Lark Rise* she looked first at the opening paragraph of her essay 'An Oxfordshire Hamlet in the Eighties', which began: 'The hamlet stood on a gentle rise which in that flat corn growing part of the country was dignified by the name of "the hill," '[12] and she altered it to her now famous first lines:

> The hamlet stood on a gentle rise in the flat, wheat growing, north east corner of Oxfordshire. We will call it Lark Rise because of the great number of skylarks which made the surrounding fields their springboard and nested on the bare earth between the rows of green corn.[13]

When people asked her about her writing Flora said that she often rewrote paragraphs over and over again until she was satisfied that they were as good as she could possibly make them and had achieved the simplicity that appeared spontaneous. Her years of reading and writing verse, and of teaching the techniques of prose, had not been wasted. Her ear was perfectly attuned, her voice mature, she was at last writing from the best that she was and it was very good.

She had set out from her Oxfordshire home on a May morning when she was fourteen, between then and her sixtieth year she had travelled to other counties, she had travelled spiritually and intellectually, but like all the best journeys hers was a circular one and she returned for renewal to the place of her birth.

When she had finished her book, Flora packed up the fifteen chapters of *Lark Rise* and sent them to Oxford University Press where Sir Humphrey Milford, Publisher to The University, instantly recognized their worth, he encouraged Flora to expand her essays into a full-length book. From then on Flora received help and encouragement from all the members of the Press's staff but her chief help and later personal friend, was Geoffrey Cumberlege, deputy to Sir Humphrey Milford. Geoffrey Cumberlege became Flora's editor. Initially Geoffrey Cumberlege had a problem; *Lark Rise*[14] appeared to be fiction and The Press did not publish fiction, but he was determined to publish Flora's book so he called it autobiography. The book was accepted in the summer of 1938 and an artist commissioned to do the illustrations; the artist was Lynton Lamb. In September 1938 he went to stay in Brackley, from where he walked to Juniper Hill each day to do the pen-and-ink drawings which were to illustrate Flora's book.

Lynton Lamb had been born in India but spent his childhood in London and his schooldays in Bath. He had studied at the Central School of Arts and Crafts before joining the staff of Oxford University Press where he worked on new designs for the bindings of the Bible and Book of Common Prayer. He had studied book binding under Douglas Cockerell whom he succeeded as a part-time lecturer at The Central in the 1930s. When he was commissioned to illustrate *Lark Rise*[15] he was thirty-one. He had already illustrated books for the private presses of the day with his wood engravings but was turning to pen-and-ink which was the medium he was to use for the *Lark Rise* pictures.

Brackley, where Lynton Lamb stayed at The Crowne Hotel, was the town to which Flora's father had walked or cycled every day of his thirty-five years as a mason. Lynton Lamb walked the same three miles each day to do his sketches. Albert Timms would have been amazed had he lived long enough, to know that an artist walked the road he hated so much, for the purpose of illustrating a book written by his eldest daughter: a book about the place he once described, as 'the spot God made with the leftovers when he had finished creating the rest of the earth'.[16]

Lynton Lamb liked Juniper Hill, he wrote to Flora from his hotel on 14 September 1938:

> You will be reassured, I imagine, to hear that I took to Juniper immediately, and if only I could stay longer and take more time I should be quite happy ... I found the first glimpse as one turns from the Oxford Road most moving. There is a queer quality about it, rather sinister, like the smell of woodsmoke from a gypsy encampment ... it is the very low tone of the colour I think, the mole-coloured thatch and the small trees dark like gorse and with drifts of white smoke over it. But to draw it. One would need to be a Rembrandt.[17]

Flora enjoyed reading that letter, it is the letter of an artist and a man deeply involved with the job in hand, his were to be no quick unconsidered sketches, his interest and humour illuminated the letter and gave her great confidence in his ability to do the book justice. His letter went on to say:

> I found Laura's cottage, and Queenie's house, sweet and small with Hollyhocks and pig noises ... Clerk Tom's cottage is there and very nice too like a little baked apple.

He reported that his arrival in the hamlet,

> ... caused quite as big a stir amongst the children I believe as your cheap jack, 'though as I lack his arts the novelty has worn off, and in any case the arrival of the school attendance officers, (one very fat in pale blue tweed coat and black bowler) has quite eclipsed any sensation I may have made.[18]

Lynton Lamb only had a few days in which to complete his work, he would have liked longer, he knew from his reading of the book that Flora too had an artist's seeing eye, and it was very

important to her that the drawings recalled the real *Lark Rise*.[19]
At the end of his long and kindly letter he wrote:

> I do hope you may find some remnants of your Juniper in my
> drawings. I have no time to stand and stare and also have to work
> in pen-and-ink (a hard and rather slick medium) but I think they
> will be more selective than photographs.[20]

The result of his work was ten drawings of a Juniper Hill
almost unchanged since Flora's childhood. When he came to
look for the end house, Lynton Lamb decided that he much
preferred the cottage in which Flora was born. The end house
was, and is still, a very small, plain building; Flora's birthplace
was a picturesque thatched double cottage. In a letter to her
sister May, sent with a copy of *Lark Rise*, Flora wrote, 'I really
intended the end house to be the one you were born in and in
which we lived so long, but the picture facing page seven is of
that old house round the hill I was born in.'[21]

Sadly the pretty thatched cottage was demolished after the
war, without Lynton Lamb's drawing there would be no record
of it. The drawing was reproduced in a *New York Tribune* review
and Flora found it very strange to see the house where she was
born pictured in an American paper. Some American reviews
were sent to her as bait to get her to subscribe to a press-cutting
agency. She did not subscribe to the American agency but later
she did use an English one, she carefully preserved all her press
cuttings which eventually filled six books, ironically now in
America.

Lynton Lamb's other drawings of Juniper include
conventional views like the interior of Cottisford church which
he felt expected to do, not by Flora but by the reading public.
Others are more revealing, both of the hamlet and of the artist.
One with the caption from the text, 'games were played in the
open spaces between the cottages,' shows two bicycles leaning
against a tumbledown barn in a weedy yard. There is not a child
in sight but the picture tells all. Lynton Lamb worked without
preliminary sketches, directly onto paper with pen-and-ink and
his hasty broken lines convey his impression of Juniper Hill as
he saw it in the autumn of 1938. George Mackie in his book on
the work of Lynton Lamb[22] describes the illustrations for *Lark
Rise* as 'full of plein air, delicacy and feeling. They are also
highly accurate documents lovingly observed.'

Lynton Lamb was to go on after serving in the war, to
illustrate an impressive list of books, to design the binding of the
Bible used at the Coronation in 1952 and to design the book
jackets for the much loved World's Classics series, which was to
include Flora's trilogy. He was a painter, a lithographer and a
distinguished designer. In his own delightful book *County
Town*,[23] written after the war, Lynton Lamb likened the
returning soldier to:

> ... an illustrator reading the manuscript of a story. He goes
> through nebulous territory until some trivial fact sharpens his
> focus and sets a scale to which he can relate other experience. A
> dog in a back yard, the shafts of a trap, an iron table on which
> gardening gloves have been laid, may suddenly precipitate a
> cloudy mental state to crystal clearness.

Flora was lucky in having Lynton Lamb as her illustrator.

She was lucky too in her publisher. Geoffrey Cumberlege had
joined Oxford University Press in 1919 after serving in the First
World War and had been in charge of The Press's Indian
branch and later responsible for business in America. He was a
kindly man, a true lover of books and fine arts, endowed with
just the right combination of encouragement and tact needed in
dealing with authors. Not that Flora was a difficult author. In
later years he was to call her an easy author whose books had an
easy birth, but the circumstances of her life were still such that
she needed all his encouragement because she had a great lack
of confidence in her work. There were also to be times when
Geoffrey Cumberlege tactfully offered her extra advances of
money to tide her over until a book was ready or royalties were
due. She and John had only his Post Office pension to depend
on. The least hint of patronage would have made Flora
withdraw into her shell, but Geoffrey Cumberlege's handling of
her was faultless.

In February 1939, a month before *Lark Rise*[24] was due to be
published, Mr Cumberlege received a letter from Oxford
University Press's manager in New York, asking for more details
of the author of *Lark Rise*, which he had already read in
instalments sent over to him from England. He wrote:

> I have been reading with a great feeling of contentment the
> instalments of *Lark Rise* which have been turning up. I like it and
> am terribly glad to turn to it in spare moments. It has an amazing

English quality of permanence and repose.... I should very much like to know the history of the author. She writes with such ease that it is hard to believe she has not considerable literary experience.[25]

Geoffrey Cumberlege had to coax information about herself from Flora. 'If you will put modesty in the corner,' he wrote, 'and let me have a note about yourself, it shall be treated with such reverence as you could wish. I need hardly tell you, for I think I have done so before, what a great pleasure it is to be publishing this very charming book of yours.'[26]

Lark Rise was published in March 1939 and for a brief spell, Flora was able to enjoy the success she had worked for for a lifetime. She was used to seeing her name in print, newspapers and magazines had carried many thousands of her words but nothing before had given her the pleasure she felt on opening her door to a postman offering her a parcel containing copies of her first work between hard covers, a real book at last. But already her joy was tinged with fear, there was talk of war again and she had a twenty-year-old son just finishing his apprenticeship as a ship's engineer.

Despite the threatening news from abroad Flora was pleased when the reviews reached her in Dartmouth, they were very good. *Country Life* gave it pride of place on their book review page of 25 March. The reviewer, Edith Oliver said that Flora possessed: '... a literary gift which enables her to write, in clear precise and exact prose, a little masterpiece of description.'

The *Yorkshire Post* called her book: 'a lovely cameo';[27] *Time and Tide*: 'A remarkable picture of village life.'[28] *The Sunday Times* said: 'it can claim the rank of an historical document,'[29] and *The Times Literary Supplement* in May featured *Lark Rise*[30] as social history. *Lark Rise* is not pure social history, although there is so much social history in it that book after book written since the war, on the nineteenth century, quote from it, and 'Thompson/Flora' appears frequently in the indexes of such books.

Flora received many letters of appreciation from readers which gave her great pleasure and belies the stories that her ambitions were never fulfilled and that she died a disappointed writer. She heard from family in Oxfordshire that Lady Bicester of Tusmore House, not far from Juniper liked her books. Flora wrote to her sister, 'such praise makes mc fccl vcry humble. It is rather amusing to think of my books being read at Tusmore. Father helped to finish rebuilding that house.'[31] Flora's mother had acquired a beadcd footstool from Tusmore house when the old mansion burned down. She had coveted the little round stool with its claw feet and beaded top and was very proud of it. She and Albert could never have dreamed that a lady of Tusmore House would one day read books written by their daughter.

Flora's books have actually lasted longer than the house which Albert Timms helped to rebuild. The Victorian country mansion was demolished in the 1960s and replaced with a smaller contemporary house.

Within twenty years Flora's work was to be uscd in school text books throughout the English speaking world. The University of London was to use the trilogy in the syllabus of the 'O' level English literature course. The girl whose elementary education was not enough to allow her to take a Civil Service examination, had written a classic book, a piece of enduring English literature.

What makes *Lark Rise* so good? Defining its virtues is akin to digging up a plant to inspect its roots, hoping to see how its flower was produced. The book, like a plant, had its roots firmly in the soil and drew its strength from there. Its colour and vitality come from Flora herself, its quality from her innate integrity and her ability to observe and record her observations in pure prose.

The timing of *Lark Rise* was fortuitous. A few decades earlier, Flora would have been telling her readers about things which many of them preferred to forget; poverty, pig killing, sterner moral values, but in the uncertain world of 1939 the 1880s had stability which held great appeal. The appeal was not a sweet, sentimental nostalgia; through Laura's eyes Flora saw everything as it had been and gave her readers a book they could believe in. The lack of self pity felt by the people of *Lark Rise* commanded respect. Women particularly, read of the lives of the *Lark Rise* wives and mothers and weighed their roles against those of their own time. Flora rarely judged or drew conclusions, she simply described what had happened, resisting the temptation to comment with hindsight.

H.J. Massingham was later to describe the book as: ' ... of

great complexity and heavy with revolutionary meaning'.[32] He felt that Flora had depicted the utter ruin of a closely knit organic society. That too is one of the secrets of the book. Whilst seeming to paint a picture of a safe unchanging world, Flora depicted change as imperceptible as growth. The story has many layers and however many times the book is read, something new will be seen. *Lark Rise*, like life, goes on happening.

15 War Time

All through 1939 Flora worked on *Over to Candleford*, continuing to mine the rich vein of her memories. Day by day in her home above the estuary of the River Dart, Flora wrote an evocation of a country town in the peaceful days of the 1880s.

1939 was not a year of peace. In September the unthinkable happened, war was declared and Flora found herself a spectator of events which threatened those she loved. Her daughter who was on holiday in Switzerland when war was declared, got home just in time, Basil and his family were safely settled in Australia. When the war was only one week old Flora wrote to her daughter-in-law in Australia, 'The world already seems a different place, Dartmouth is very empty and black as a tomb at night.'[1]

Flora began to find it difficult to make time for her writing. It took her a whole week to make blackout curtains from Peter's old camping blankets, because there was no black material to be found in any of the Dartmouth shops. John was busy all day and sometimes all night on ARP (air-raid precautions) work. Flora's contribution to the war effort was to take his telephone messages when he was out, on the telephone they had specially installed. She had last had to do telephone duties in the Post Office in Liphook in the 1914–18 war. Peter worked until nine or ten each night at the shipyard, where they were busy with new orders. Winifred went back to the maternity home in Bristol where she felt that her work with mothers and babies as important as war nursing, much to Flora's relief.

Flora's life at this time was lonely but she was no longer strong and she dreaded the thought of having to accommodate evacuees. She had just enough energy to cope with looking after her husband and son with all the difficulties of rationing and wartime restrictions. She began to need help in the house as her health deteriorated, but domestic help became impossible to find in wartime. So Flora worked on, combining cleaning, washing, shopping and cooking with her writing and all with diminishing strength.

Flora's great friend Mildred Humble-Smith with whom she had run the Peverel Society had sons in uniform, Roger who was Peter's age, joined the Royal Navy, Anthony, two years younger was in the RAF. The two women had run their postal writers' circle since 1925, reading and commenting on the many hundreds of manuscripts which travelled the country in their portfolios. They had written courses on literary techniques and helped many amateur writers to achieve publication, but Flora was finding it difficult to make time for the society now that her own work was so successful. Both women guessed that their members would soon be too preoccupied with war work to write, and they began to consider disbanding the society for the duration of the war.

Resolutely Flora worked on outlining the contents of *Over to Candleford*[2] in a letter to Geoffrey Cumberlege, who wrote straight back in October offering her the same terms for the book as for *Lark Rise* without even seeing it, he wrote, 'We all hope you will push on with it as hard as you can and let us have it as soon as possible.'[3]

Flora and John realized early in the war that they were living in a very vulnerable place. Dartmouth with its deep harbour, its shipyards and the Royal Naval College, was going to be a prime target for the enemy, so they began to look for another home. Flora had grown to love Dartmouth and was sorry to leave it, but she was getting older, the terrain was steep, and the waters of the river below her windows were now busy with wartime activity, a sight not conducive to a quiet mind and she needed quiet to recollect her memories. Her friend Mrs Christine Tylor had already left Dartmouth when Dr Tylor retired.

Basil, Winifred and Peter had all left home, and there was little to tie her to Dartmouth. Then Peter, her youngest and dearest child was drawn into the war. He joined the merchant navy and it was soon obvious to everyone that merchant shipping was at risk.

In November and December of that year Flora struggled to continue *Over to Candleford*, but then she almost gave up. She wrote to Mr Cumberlege in January offering to return the advance already paid on the book. Characteristically he remained gently encouraging, 'Write the book in your own time,' he told her in a letter, 'it will always be welcome here and you are still extremely welcome to the advance that has been paid to you. No promise has been broken because the war has upset everybody's calculations.'

John had retired from the Post Office in 1935 but the war gave him new work to do, he was an ARP warden and acted as a house agent, renting and selling property. Flora was glad that he had found an outlet for his business ability, a bored husband about the house would have been a worry and a hindrance to her. Instead John was out and busy every day, happy to bring home fresh-caught fish and cook it for their meal. Without his help *Over to Candleford* might not have been finished.

After looking at houses all through the winter of 1939 and early 1940, Flora and John found a house they liked in Brixham five miles away. Property was not easy to find in south Devon during the war. Brixham had become home to many Belgian fishing families who had fled to England after the invasion of their own country. The Thompsons befriended a Belgian family, their friendship lasting until the war ended.

Flora and John bought their new home in Brixham in March 1940. The house, Lauriston, is an old cottage built end-on to the hillside, hidden from the sea and the town centre. There is an attractive early nineteenth-century veranda on the front of the house which gives it a considerable resemblance to a house which Flora described in an unfinished novel written in Brixham and called *Dashpers*.[4]

Lauriston was a roomy house for a retired couple and one which allowed Flora to turn a spare room into a study. She kept books in every room and furnished her new home with the small treasures she loved, pretty china and small antiques. John added buying antiques on commission for a shop owner to his business activities when prices rose, as antiques were in demand as alternatives to utility furnishings. Flora then mourned that she could no longer get any of her nice little bargains.

Lauriston had a very large cellar, which was to come in useful when Brixham had its share of air raid alerts. Higher up the hill, the garden was approached by a flight of steps and is long, level and walled which made it very private. After life in a road of semi-detached houses in Dartmouth, Lauriston was wonderfully withdrawn. Geoffrey Cumberlege hoped that, 'The cottage will be pleasant and chatter free, so that you may have the quiet you need for your writing.'[5] A vain hope in wartime.

After the evacuation of Dunkirk, to which the town of Brixham sent about a dozen ships, France fell in June 1940 and the Germans occupied the French coast and the Channel Islands. The coast of Devon began to suffer air attacks, but despite the disturbances of war, and her fears for Peter out on the Atlantic, Flora managed to finish *Over to Candleford* and the proofs were ready by February 1941.

Everyone at Oxford University Press thought the new book delightful, their only criticism was that it was too short. This time there were no illustrations beyond a little drawing on the jacket and the title page done by an artist who was not even able to read the whole book. Lynton Lamb was serving in the Royal Engineers, working on camouflage, the war made everything difficult. Early editions of the book had a dropped word on the first page, Geoffrey Cumberlege mentioning it in a letter to Flora said, 'I suppose that word is really a war casualty. Considering conditions I think the book has turned out nicely, and of course as a piece of literature it is wholly delightful.'[6]

Flora herself thought *Over to Candleford* lightweight and seems not to have been altogether happy with it, the critics and the public had no such reservations: 'An air of quiet enchantment broods over the narrative, so artful is the concealment of art. This is rural England, unadulterated, fresh on the palate as summer lettuces or peas' was the *Observer*'s review.[7] *The Spectator*'s reviewer commented that Flora had written of her childhood with a proud care not to romanticize.[8] *Punch* said that reading *Over to Candleford* was like looking through a cottage window into a life countrified and peaceful. Flora had written the perfect book for readers in wartime, a book to remind them of better days. *The Times Literary Supplement*'s reviewer said: 'We are given no more about the further influences which breathed on this little village girl ... and which turned her into a woman who could look back with serenity and exquisite detachment to a rigorous childhood in an obscure village and from it distil this very essence of English life.'[9]

In *Over to Candleford* Flora took her readers into an English market town. She told enquirers that Candleford was mostly Buckingham, the home of her father's family, with something of Banbury in her picture too. The contrasts between life in the hamlet and the town are shown in so many subtle ways that the reader is hardly aware of how the contrast is made, and only knows that it is. The world is seen through Laura's eyes, yet with a lifetime of Flora's discernment in her gaze.

Everyone wanted to know more about what happened to Laura. Geoffrey Cumberlege wrote, 'If you have another book in you don't hesitate to start getting it out of your system and on to paper.'[10]

She had written one successful sequel why not another? All the reviews which appeared in the summer of 1941 were full of praise, even Flora, so lacking in personal confidence could see that readers loved her work. She had achieved her lifelong ambition, a real literary success which celebrated and shared more of her country childhood. But her happiness was short lived.

On 16 September a telegram was delivered to Lauriston, Peter's ship *The Jedmoor*, carrying a cargo of wheat across the Atlantic, had been topedoed, only six men were saved, Peter, just twenty-two, was not one of them. Flora wrote to Geoffrey Cumberlege, 'He was our youngest, a latecomer and tenderly loved. That there are thousands of mothers and wives suffering as I am only seems to make it harder to bear.'[11] Her friend Mildred Humble-Smith also lost a son at sea, Roger Humble-Smith died on the Murmansk run. The two bereaved mothers immediately disbanded the Peverel Society. Flora needed all her courage to cope with her loss, although her daughter Winifred was later to say that the old country expression, 'She never flinched', most certainly applied to her.

To ease her sorrow Flora went on working. Since finishing *Over to Candleford* she had been writing the book she called

Dashpers,[12] the story of a house and those who lived in it. In October she sent a chapter to Oxford University Press with an outline of the plot. Geoffrey Cumberlege replied, 'I think there is nothing more to say than carry on.' There was, however, a hint of uncertainty about this book in his letter. 'I am sure we shall like it although it will, of course, be rather different to the other two.'

But circumstances were against *Dashpers*. That winter Flora became ill. The combination of sorrow, the privations of war and perhaps overwork, had made her vulnerable. She developed pneumonia and was ill in bed for some weeks. She was slow to recover and when she did she was never strong again.

In the spring of 1942 when she began to write again, she did not continue with *Dashpers* which she left at chapter three. Instead she began a new book which she called *Candleford Green*,[13] a story about another part of rural life, the village. She had already given her readers a taste of village life in the chapter on Candleford Green in her last book. Now she decided to develop the story. To please readers who asked what happened to Laura, she began to remember the days when she had left home to work in a village Post Office.

She wrote under enormous difficulty. Dartmouth, only five miles away, suffered heavy bombing and Brixham had many day-time attacks when hit-and-run raiders attacked the shipyard where over 1,000 vessels were built or repaired during the war. The Royal Naval College at Dartmouth was bombed, as was the shipyard, Phillips at Noss. The loss of life and injuries suffered there, when workshops full of heavy machinery were blown apart were appalling. Many of the men killed or injured had worked with Peter. The news was a double blow to Flora, who realized that had her son stayed in his civilian job he might still have been a casualty of war.

In a world which seemed to be destroying itself Flora worked on, creating quietly despite war and destruction. It was all she could do. She was too old and unwell to do any sort of war work, so she did what she was best at, she recreated a past which gave people anchors for the present. Perhaps it was only by immersing herself in that other, kindlier world, that she was able to carry on. Food and fuel were in short supply, life was hard for everyone, each developed their own defences, Flora's was work. Sometimes when the siren sounded she had to pick up her typescript and take it into the Morrison shelter in her cellar, where she worked to the sound of bombs falling.

She allowed only one intimation of the threatening times in which she lived to appear in the book. In the chapter entitled 'The Green', she described how she had watched boys one evening in the 1890s, flying kites to which they had fixed lighted candle ends:

> The little lights floated and flickered like fireflies against the dusk of the sky and the darker tree tops. It was a pretty sight, although, perhaps, the sport was a dangerous one, for one of the kites caught fire and came down as tinder. At that, some men, drinking their pints outside the inn door for coolness, rushed forward and put a stop to it. Madness they called it, stark staring madness, and asked the youths if they wanted to set the whole place on fire. But how innocent and peaceful compared with our present menace from the air.[14]

In a letter to one of her sisters Flora wrote, 'What a world we live in. The old days were paradise compared to these, if only we had been able to appreciate them.'[15]

In *Candleford Green* Flora commented on the changes she had seen happening when she was in her teens in Fringford. People in the village were better off than those she had known in Juniper Hill but she saw that, spiritually they had lost ground, rather than gained it.

Country people had been faced by a choice, to merge with the new mass standards, or adapt the best of the new to their own needs, a choice which Flora felt in 1942 still had to be determined. At the end of the book Flora told how Laura disappeared from the country scene, but remained bound to her native county by threads, 'Spun of love and kinship and cherished memories.'[16]

Candleford Green was finally published in January 1943. It received magnificent reviews. *The Times Literary Supplement* said: 'Miss Thompson's readers have coalesced into a faithful band of followers of what promises to be an unusual series, we wait, impatient for the next instalment.'[17]

Even in America people wanted more, the *Book Review Digest* reviewer said: 'I put the book down feeling refreshed and wanting very much to know what will happen to Laura, in Flora Thompson's next instalment.' The *New York Times* which had reviewed Flora's first two books said: 'Flora Thompson has begun something that, when completed should form a source book from which future historians may draw with utter confidence. It is the drama of life untinged by meretricious glamour and seen, clear-eyed by a realist of poetic temperament.'[18]

Only H.J. Massingham, writing in *Time and Tide*[19] seems to have realized that Flora had in fact already completed something, that no further instalments were appropriate. In his review he refers to the three books as a trilogy, although the idea of producing them as such was only just being discussed between Flora and her publishers. His long and perceptive review brought the three books together under the claim that they would be ' ... regarded by posterity as of permanent significance.' H.J. Massingham read far more into all three of Flora's books than most other reviewers, Massingham wrote: 'In her shell we hear the thunder of an ocean of change, a change tragic indeed since nothing has taken and nothing can take the place of what has gone. A design for living has become unravelled.'[20]

Geoffrey Cumberlege wrote to Flora to make sure that she had read the *Time and Tide* review. His letter contained congratulations and the suggestion, 'One day we must talk about the trilogy and meanwhile you must let me know what plans you have for future books.'[21]

Flora was tired in 1943. She had filled the two years since Peter's death with hard work. The war dragged on and for a time she wrote nothing new. Geoffrey Cumberlege wrote to her, 'I am afraid you have had a disturbed winter and have suffered from the German game of tip and run. Nevertheless with this warm spring you will be beginning to feel the urge to write.'[22]

At first Flora responded by offering to finish *Dashpers* but Mr Cumberlege still had doubts about it, 'I like everything you write,' he said, 'but I do not think this shows you at your happiest.'[23] Next Flora sent him some of her old 'Peverel Papers' and suggested that perhaps she could put them together as a book. That idea met with a more enthusiastic response. 'The Peverel Papers are full of good things,' Geoffrey Cumberlege wrote in March 1943, 'and I am sure you can do such a book as you describe extremely well. It would be nice if you could let us see a little bit of the book as soon as it has begun to take shape. But I can tell you here and now that we shall be delighted to publish it.'[24] This idea was never brought to fruition by Flora; over thirty years were to elapse before 'Peverel Papers' appeared in hard covers.

Paper and printing were becoming a great problem, all books had to be produced in line with the authorized war economy standard, which often meant that they were printed on wafer-thin paper which yellowed rapidly. Geoffrey Cumberlege worked hard to keep up Oxford University Press's standards of good-book production but Flora's books had suffered progressively from wartime economies, *Lark Rise* was a large, well-illustrated book, *Over to Candleford* was diminished in size and illustrated only on the cover and the title page, *Candleford Green* suffered even more from war economy standards. The idea of producing all three books as a trilogy, not only put them together as the complete piece of literature which they undoubtedly were, but saved on bindings.

During the summer of 1943 Flora was touched to receive a letter from her nephew Leslie, the son of her youngest sister Annie. Leslie had read his aunt's books and wrote to tell her how much he had enjoyed them. Flora replied and began a correspondence which lasted until her death. Aunt and nephew were to meet and become good friends. Flora enjoyed contact with the young and, although he could never replace her son, Leslie helped to heal Peter's loss.

Leslie Castle was a talented amateur artist; when Flora learned this she gave him much gentle encouragement and in doing so she often revealed her own feelings as a creative artist. She told him,

Any art work needs time and patience and needs above all a quiet mind. I think yours is a lovely art. I adore colour. All arts are similar, there is a good deal of time and patience needed for writing if it is to turn out a success. I write my books several times over, revising every paragraph, entirely remoulding many until I get them, not as good as I should like them to be, but the best it is in me to do.[25]

When wartime duties made life difficult for her nephew she wrote, 'How is your painting going on? Not much time or opportunity I fear away from home, but cherish all new impressions, they will come back to you in better days and all help feed your inspiration.'[26]

Flora's comments about the arts showed her to have been vitally interested in creativity. She was very aware that it had taken her a lifetime to find her own voice, she commented sadly to her nephew, 'Art is long but life is short.'[27]

The only art form which she could not fully appreciate was music but she viewed her loss with her usual wry humour; in one letter to her nephew she wrote,

> Music too is a beautiful art and one which I think appeals to a much greater number of people than any of the other arts. Unfortunately, and I have always felt it a great loss, I am rather in the position of the man who said he could never distinguish between *God Save The Weasel* and *Pop Goes The King*, but I always envy those who can appreciate good music. They are lucky in these days of broadcasting. Poetry I love and all good literature and next to that your own art of painting, it is a lovely art and one of which I have often envied its possessors when words have seemed too pale and cold a medium.[28]

In the winter of 1943 Geoffrey Cumberlege went to Edinburgh to look for printers and binders who could take on more work: English printers were working to capacity and there was a tremendous desire for books in wartime. People read to take their minds from wartime problems and to alleviate boredom. Books were read by lonely firewatchers, worried women, travelling soldiers: people everywhere read more than they had done in peacetime. Books like Flora's, were particularly popular because of the reassuring nature of the English scene they depicted.

Flora was in need of reassurance too. She still felt unwell and began to express doubts that she would live to see the trilogy published. As ever, Geoffrey Cumberlege's kindness was directed at her self doubt. They had become good friends by then, they met in Devon and talked books and Flora began to search for out-of-print books for his collection. It was a service she had performed for some Peverel Society members, as part of their common interest in literature. Flora enjoyed searching the shelves of antiquarian and second-hand bookshops for treasures.

Geoffrey Cumberlege was a keen book collector and was at

that time collecting the Cranford series of classic books, which had been published in the eighties and nineties, illustrated by Hugh Thompson and Charles Brock. They were beautiful books, bound in green and decorated lavishly with gold. Geoffrey Cumberlege was looking for Thackeray's *The Virginians* to go with the copy of *Esmond* which he had already. Flora had a copy of *The Virginians* which she sent to him with a letter in which she wrote, '*The Virginians*, like most sequels of famous books, is as water unto wine after *Esmond*, but it is very good water with a delightful Thackerayish flavour and well worth sipping.'

Geoffrey Cumberlege was to say years later that Flora Thompson's book-finding service for her friends was never a businesslike affair, since she much preferred to give what she had at some cost found, or charge less for the book than the postage cost. When she sent *The Virginians* to Mr Cumberlege she wrote, 'If you care to keep it and are not willing to accept it as a mouthful of hay for your hobby I think five shillings would be a fair price.'[29]

Mr and Mrs Cumberlege worried about Flora's health. In the same letter Flora wrote, 'Please thank dear Mrs Cumberlege for her kind enquiry about the food and tell her that I am not doing too badly at present as I am allowed a daily pint of priority milk and get an extra egg occasionally.' She thanked Mrs Cumberlege too for some tea which she had sent to her, ' ... a rare luxury in these days and her kind thought in sending it makes it doubly refreshing.'[30]

Although John was now concerned for Flora's frail state of health, she had had very little cherishing in her life and few friends with whom she could share her love of literature. She responded to Mr and Mrs Cumberlege with characteristic shy warmth, her contacts with them were small gleams of light in otherwise dark days.

Flora still missed Ronald Macfie, he had been her main link with the literary world. When she wrote to console her nephew after he lost a friend she said, 'I know well what a blank such losses mean, the chief friend of my life was a Scotsman Dr Ronald Macfie and I lost him by death ten years ago, a loss never to be replaced.' She added, 'You are young and the years will bring many interesting friends into your life. The difficulty is I know, to find them with the same interests and ideas as yourself. The truth of the matter is that anyone at all out of the ordinary has always a rather lonely life.'[31]

Flora's lonely struggle to write in wartime went on, but the war intruded more and more. She commented in a letter to her nephew, 'The peace and quiet so essential to any artistic work is a thing of the past. It is a sad world and I think a mad world we live in today and the only comfort is the knowledge that it cannot remain so forever.'[32]

The war was to end in a year, but during that year Flora found herself surrounded by a gathering invasion force. Brixham, like most of the south coast, was almost under siege at this time, as plans for the D-Day landings went ahead and the assault craft assembled. An exercise to rehearse the landings took place on nearby Slapton Sands with tragic results: 700 American troops drowned when 9 German E-boats slipped through naval defences in the dark and sank three fully loaded landing craft.

In Brixham special concrete slipways were constructed to allow tanks and other vehicles to be loaded into landing vessels. Shortly before D-Day, three houses near the harbour were requisitioned with only five days' notice for the families who lived in them to move out, before their homes were demolished to allow an easier passage for the huge US Army tanks manoeuvring into place. In Dartmouth GIs were dropped from lorries in Above Town, close to Flora's old home, where they streamed across the fields and down roads towards the landing craft. These troops were destined to land on Utah beach in Normandy.

Flora, like most local people, knew that something important was happening but all were forbidden to talk or write about events. At the time of the D-Day preparations all public transport in Brixham was halted, as the US Army vehicles queued nose-to-tail on the roads leading to the sea.

Unable to walk in peace or safety during the late spring days of 1944, Flora thought about a sequel to *Candleford Green*, one which would tell the continuing story of her Post Office career.

16   The Open Book

After spending the years since the outbreak of war writing about Oxfordshire, Flora longed to go back and see her old home. She was well-known enough by 1944 to be invited to speak about her books to a group of Oxfordshire librarians[1] but she could not go. Wartime travel was difficult and she was in poor health. Besides which she felt that she could never screw up enough courage to address the librarians, she told her nephew Leslie that she was a poor talker and shy as a mouse. Flora may have lacked the confidence for public speaking but she was not shy when talking to individuals, she was too keenly interested in others to be shy. She turned down the invitation to speak to the librarians but continued to hope for a trip to Juniper one day: 'I am looking forward to visiting Oxfordshire after the war is over and shall hope to see everybody belonging to me,' she wrote in the winter of 1944.

Plans for the publication of the trilogy were going ahead; her books were very popular and Oxford University Press were keen to get them out under one cover despite the difficulties of labour and paper shortage.

A young wood engraver Julie Neild was commissioned to do the illustrations for the book. She wrote to Flora asking her for details of cottage interiors and the clothes worn by country people sixty years earlier. She received kindly replies which helped her to produce her engravings. Flora's natural good taste and considerable knowledge of illustrated books made her a sound judge of successful illustrations. By March Flora had received the first proofs of the engravings by registered post for her approval.

Julie Neild held down a daytime war job and worked on the wood engravings in the evening. She had been aware of wood engraving in childhood, her father knew Eric Gill and David Jones, so when she had the opportunity to learn the craft she did so, eventually training at The Ruskin School of drawing in Oxford where Eric Ravilious was a visiting lecturer of wood engraving, lettering and graphic design.

In the 1930s and forties there were many excellent women wood engravers at work, such as Joan Hassall, Clare Leighton and Gwen Raverat. Julie Neild's engravings are a delightful evocation of rural life in the 1880s. Despite the small scale of the illustrations, she put great detail into each block, 'a kettle sings on the hob', 'a tinker's brazier smokes on a cart loaded with grindstones', etc. Julie Neild was not able to visit Juniper Hill in wartime but she studied the text very carefully and researched the period.

Some of the illustrations are not scenes but details; a lace pillow hung with bobbins, the Buckinghamshire lace making a background pattern, or wood-working tools entwined with wood shavings. Each block compliments the text and in the first editions of the trilogy, despite wartime economies, they printed well.

As soon as Oxford University Press received the wood blocks, they made zincotype line blocks which would stand up better than boxwood to repeated printings. This was fortunate, as the wood blocks were a casualty of the London Blitz.

The next step in putting the trilogy together was to have an introduction written. For this Geoffrey Cumberlege approached H.J. Massingham who had written such a perceptive review of *Candleford Green* in *Time and Tide*. In July 1944 Geoffrey Cumberlege was able to write to tell Flora that he had accepted, 'He says that I am to tell you that he is much honoured by the invitation. I hope you will find this good news cheering.'[2] It was indeed good news.

Harold John Massingham was a popular and discerning

writer on rural subjects. He had been a journalist in London until ill-health forced him to live in the country where he wrote a weekly column for *The Field*. He also wrote a long list of country books himself, he was a passionate advocate of mixed farming and supporter of country crafts and the English character. He prophesied ecological disaster, factory farming, the ills caused by over-refined foods and much else, which is today accepted but which, when he was writing, earned him the label of a reactionary.

In his choice of H.J. Massingham, Geoffrey Cumberlege was as perceptive as ever. Flora was greatly reassured to find that at last, someone fully understood her aims in writing. She wrote to thank Massingham for agreeing to write the introduction saying, 'I feel I must tell you what a very great pleasure this good news has given me. I feel highly honoured that you should be willing to stand godfather to my simple records and I am pleased and relieved to know that my offspring is now assured of kind and sympathetic treatment.'[3]

It is typical of Flora that she saw Massingham, not as a literary man asked to praise her work, but as godfather to her offspring, a truly country compliment. In another letter to him Flora wrote, 'Words as to the inner emotions do not come readily to me, for I have led an isolated life mentally and spiritually ... reviewers have been kind and I have had a few letters of appreciation from readers, no one but you has recognised my aims and intentions in writing of that more excellent way of life of our forefathers.'[4]

She seems to have felt that readers and reviewers took the three separate volumes of her work at face value, enjoying the nostalgic pictures she had created simply as escapist reading. With H.J. Massingham's introduction, she hoped that the reading public might now see what she was trying to achieve and gain a deeper understanding of what had been so recently lost from English rural life.

The introduction to the trilogy is as well worth reading as the books which follow it, drawing together as it does all the elements which go to make up the fabric of Flora's triune achievement. Massingham's knowledge of social history enabled him to see beyond the outline of the three stories, of the hamlet, the village and the town, to the historic causes of the conditions which Flora had observed so accurately. He realized that Flora, like Jane Austen, whom she admired so much, wrote well not in spite of rural seclusion, but because of it. He wrote: 'Her art is in fact universalised by its very particularity, its very confinement to small places and the people who Laura knew.'

Each of Flora's three books had been reprinted despite the problems of wartime and had run to four editions. Now that the trilogy was being printed, Geoffrey Cumberlege was bitterly regretting that, because of the paper shortage, it would not be ready for Christmas 1944, although he knew that the whole of the first edition would sell out very quickly. *Lark Rise to Candleford* would have made a perfect Christmas present for lovers of country books.

At this time Flora was writing her sequel to *Candleford Green* which followed Laura's progress further. So many readers and reviewers still wanted to know, 'what happened next,' that she felt forced to attempt the next instalment. She left a gap between the point at which *Candleford Green* closed with her exit from Fringford and her arrival in Grayshott, to which she gave the fictional name of *Heatherley*. Why she chose not to chronicle the short period when she moved around various Post Office jobs we shall never know. It is a sad gap which leaves *Heatherley* without a proper link to the previous books. Like its predecessors the book was the story of her own life lightly disguised, and the portrait of an era, the one which had been called at the time, *fin de siècle*. Using the techniques she had already used so well in her first three books, Flora pictured a small community, its tradesmen, the changes which were taking place and, as usual in Flora's work, there were portraits of women drawn with affection and objectivity.

For some reason Flora was not happy with *Heatherley* and she never submitted it to her publishers. As a sequel to the trilogy its failings may owe more to the place she described than to her portrait of it. Grayshott was a settlement of even more recent growth than Juniper Hill and it owed its growth, not to agricultural changes but to property development in the area, which had become popular just before Flora went there; so the social changes which she again observed and chronicled, were not rooted in the soil and the past, but in recent fashion.

As an instalment in the story of Flora's life, it has charm and interest but she never wanted to write an autobiography. Her artistic integrity told her that something was lacking in *Heatherley* and it was not published until thirty years after her death.

The winter before the trilogy appeared was a hard one, even Brixham had snow and ice which made the roads like sheets of glass, Flora had to stay indoors which she hated, it made her feel such a prisoner. Writing to her nephew she recalled, 'What deep snows we had at Juniper, on your mother's first birthday we waded home through four feet of it, Uncle Edwin and I, thinking about the baby's birthday cake Mother had made and some oranges she had promised to get for us.'[5]

Cakes and oranges were little more than a memory in the last winter of the war. In February Flora was ill again, this time she was told that she had strained her heart. She was forbidden to go for the long country walks she loved when the weather improved, frustrated by this she exclaimed in a letter, 'What a bore it is to get old and ill.'[6]

Flora received her advance copies of *Lark Rise to Candleford* in March 1945 with the news that the entire edition of 5,000 books to be published on 12 April was sold out in advance. Immediately Flora signed a copy and returned it to Geoffrey Cumberlege writing, 'I am addressing the first copy to go out to you, to whom it owes so much.' Her first action was to acknowledge her debt to Geoffrey Cumberlege, she hardly wanted acclaim for herself, 'Twenty years ago,' she commented, 'I should have been beside myself with joy but now I am too old to care for the bubble reputation.'[7]

If Flora had any remaining doubts about the nature of her achievement, the praise called forth by the book told her what others already knew. In his introduction H.J. Massingham said that, 'Her claims on posterity can hardly be questioned,' and some, like Sir Arthur Bryant, put the book as high as *Cranford*.

The reviewers were unanimous in their praise. *Country Life*'s said: 'In my view this trilogy will take a permanent place in English letters for both its individual and social significance.'[8]

In May 1945 the war ended. For Flora, as for all who had been bereaved by the war, the VE day celebrations were painful but that summer she was cheered to have her nephew to stay at Lauriston for the first time. John got his motor boat *Sea Mew* out for the visit. *Sea Mew* had been laid up in Dartmouth for the duration of the war and had not been on the water since Peter was last at home. John took his nephew for a memorable trip up the River Dart. As a keen fisherman John was delighted to have his boat out again. Flora must have felt a pang remembering how

Peter loved *Sea Mew*.

Family life continued to heal Flora's loss, she and John now had three grandchildren in Australia, Winifred who was a busy midwife came home to Brixham for a summer holiday and Flora's sister Betty was a frequent visitor, so she had little time to grieve for the son who did not come home.

Betty Timms spent a lot of time with Flora. For many years she tried to get more of her writing published, but her one children's book remained her only literary achievement. She and Flora shared their interest in writing and looking round bookshops and curio shops together when they could.

After all her summer visitors left Flora began writing a new book, tentatively called *These Too Were Victorians*; it was to become *Still Glides the Stream*.[9] She wanted to put in it a rhyme about Oxfordshire churches which Leslie had told her, 'Bloxham for strength, Adderbury for length and Kings Sutton for beauty.' She put the saying into the mouth of a character who was a stonemason, a man who is much like her own stonemason father.

She sent a sample of the new book to Geoffrey Cumberlege, after reading it he wrote to her, 'I have been spending a delightful evening with the first chapter. We all like Charity Finch both in name and character and Clerk Savings is another inspiration. It all rings true and if you keep it up to this level, as you will, you need have no fear that you will not satisfy your devotees, I congratulate you.'[10] He went on to offer her an advance of £50 and typing paper which was still in short supply and probably difficult for her to buy locally.

Flora was still corresponding with Christine Tylor who then lived in Crediton. In September Flora wrote to her, 'It was nice of you to re-read *Candleford Green* a great compliment to me as a writer. I really must try to get on with my new book this winter, though not about Laura it is about the same old Oxfordshire people, but alas, it hangs fire, so many other things to do and to see to.'[11]

Flora was pleased to learn that there were plans to bring out a Guild Books edition of *Lark Rise*,[12] one third of which were destined for Australia and the other Dominions. Her son and his family were in Australia, as was her brother Frank and his family. John Thompson had a sister working in South Africa, so it was of interest to them to know that Flora's books were being exported.

Flora saw Christine Tylor that summer, in a letter written after they met she wrote,

> I so much enjoyed that lovely afternoon we had with you. It was
> wonderful to see the old scenes once more and in such luxury. I
> feel ashamed of my lapses though, you must put them down to
> old age and to my hermit life here, I really go out so seldom that I
> feel quite lost when I do ... 'I a stranger and afraid/In a world I
> never made'[13] sort of feeling. But I know you understand.

The quotation from A.E. Housman betrays Flora's feelings
about the world in which she found herself, feelings she also
mentioned in another letter, in which she felt, 'The very
foundations of the world seem to be rocking.' The age of the
atomic bomb was a world away from *Lark Rise* and yet the
changes had all happened in her lifetime. However, despite her
fears she still enjoyed the books Christine Tylor lent her,
Charles Lamb, Fanny Burney and W.H. Hudson, her love of
literature never deserted her.

The West Country had snow again in the winter of 1945,
Flora heard that Dartmoor was white, she wrote to Leslie that
she would have loved to see it from a bus with two hot water
bottles, a fur coat and fur leggings, 'That's what I have come to,'
she said wryly, 'there was a time when I should have loved to
face the cold and wind alone in one of the most inaccessible
spots.'[14] She longed for the return of the flowers, although in
her sheltered garden she had been able to find one red rose to
put beside Peter's photograph at Christmas.

Meanwhile Flora's work on her new book was still slow, and
for a while it stopped when she was again ill in bed in the spring
of 1946. She told Mrs Tylor in a letter,

> I collapsed with a terrific attack of angina and the doctor has
> been keeping me in bed ever since for a complete rest. I am glad
> to say I have completely recovered though still feel a bit weak and
> am hoping to get out in the sun for a little tomorrow. Indeed in
> some ways I feel better than I did before the attack and am
> longing to get back to work again.[15]

Flora's illness was not helped by the times in which she lived.
Although the war was over, life was still austere, food supplies
actually diminished that year and bread was rationed for the first
time. Age, sadness and austerity were too much for Flora's frail

health. When she was ill, it was John who wrote to Geoffrey Cumberlege in reply to his enquiry about the progress of the new book. He told him that the doctor had insisted that Flora stayed in bed which she had found very irksome as she wanted to get on with her new book. Mr Cumberlege replied with characteristic concern and an offer of practical help, 'You must not allow the typing of your book to be an urgency,' he wrote, 'the only urgent thing is that you should get well. Why not send the rough material to me here so that I may get it typed?'[16]

Many years later Geoffrey Cumberlege was to say that perhaps Flora had been pressed too hard to complete *Still Glides the Stream*, 'When health and happiness were for her in short supply,' but his gentle encouraging pressure can only have had a positive effect. What worried him later, was that he felt that *Still Glides the Stream* was a rather slight sequel to *Lark Rise to Candleford*, but in that, he was comparing a good book, to a great one.

With the warmer weather Flora's health improved and she continued writing. During this time an old member of the Peverel Society went to Brixham and called on Flora. He was impressed by the woman he met, a woman of resolution and inner strength. Despite her recent illness he found her, 'Free from absorption in self or self pity, it was all in the other direction, a vital eager interest in the people she was talking to.'[17] Flora's life had moulded a character of great independence, she was reserved, ironic, down-to-earth and at-the same time, gentle. She was by then that least romantic of all human figures an old woman, but those who met her knew her to be remarkable.

Flora can no longer have doubted her own achievement, after reading a piece in Oxford University Press's book magazine, *The Periodical*,[18] in which Sir Humphrey Milford was asked which he considered the most important new book published during his thirty-two years as publisher to the university. He chose two books, A.J. Toynbee's *Study of History* and *Lark Rise to Candleford*. The writer commented that whilst Professor Toynbee's work was one of cosmic sweep and Flora's had more modest grace, both dealt in the history behind history; the style of both had that rare quality to enlighten, to entrance, to excite which distinguishes masterpieces whether they have the monumentality of *The Decline And Fall* or the fragility of *Cranford*. Flora was amazed and humbled to see her work described in such terms.

In the summer Flora wrote wistfully of her desire to see her old home again. 'I can imagine,' she wrote, 'how lovely in its quiet way that part of the country is looking now with the elder and dog roses out in the hedges and the crops coming on in the fields.'[19]

Her angina prevented Flora from taking country walks now so she sat in her garden, John was a keen gardener and kept a good succession of flowers. Although Flora had always preferred a jug of wild flowers to a formal arrangement, she had her own way of using garden blooms. On a low table in the house she liked to set a glass bowl full of water on which she floated flower heads, in a pattern which reminded her of the old Juniper Hill game of making a Pin-a-Sight, a picture made with flower petals between pieces of glass.

That summer John reluctantly decided to sell *Sea Mew*, he felt that he was getting too old to be out at sea alone. They were both sad to part with the little motor boat; Peter had loved her and they had all had many happy trips in her. But the boat was bought by the sea scouts and Flora was pleased to think of another generation of boys learning to handle her.

In July Winifred came home again for a fortnight, so with a trained nurse in the house to look after Flora, John took the opportunity to have a holiday. He travelled by coach to Bournemouth where he stayed with friends and looked up old cronies of his Post Office days. Flora, who was feeling better caught up with some reading, Mrs Tylor sent her copies of *The Spectator*, *The Countryman* and *The Times Literary Supplement*. In a letter to Christine Tylor she discussed books about the Brontës, 'It is nice of you to see some resemblance between Charlotte and me,' she wrote,[20] 'others have imagined that our faces were a little alike, I fear that we are very far apart in the things which matter.'

These Too Were Victorians was finished by August 1946 and Geoffrey Cumberlege read it and enjoyed it. He felt that it would sell well and regretted that it could not be published sooner, but the post-war period was still one of shortages and as he wrote to Flora, 'The difficulty of producing books at the present time is very great.' They were both unsure about the title which was unwieldy and not entirely appealing. 'I will think a bit more about the title,'[21] Geoffrey Cumberlege wrote on 6 August. By 17 August the book had as its title a quotation from Wordsworth's *River Duddon*, 'Still glides the stream and shall forever glide.' The title seems to have been Flora's choice but Geoffrey Cumberlege approved wholeheartedly, he wrote, 'I feel that it expresses the character of the book.'

Still Glides the Stream is set in Restharrow, Flora's fictitious name for a village not far from her mother's old home at Ardley. Restharrow is thought by some devotees to be Stoke Lyne, others think it may be Hethe but like many of Flora's places it is a composite picture of villages she knew. *Still Glides the Stream* is more like a novel than *Lark Rise to Candleford*, having the excitement of a fire at the farm, the mystery of some anonymous letters and romance. But, like its predecessors, it is mainly an evocation of rural life in the 1880s. The main character, Charity Finch is a retired teacher who revisits her old home and relives her childhood. Flora's description of her is an attractive one:

> Women of her type are not uncommon in that part of the country, they serve you in shops, nurse you in hospitals, and welcome and make you comfortable at inns. Often, as cleaners or caretakers, they show you round churches or other old buildings. They have good memories and can tell those interested where in the neighbourhood the rarer birds or less common wildflowers are to be found. They can relate, and very well, the history of an old mansion or family, or describe and sometimes interpret, a local custom ... chance met strangers have been known to unfold for them the stories of their lives.[22]

Flora herself would have made a good school teacher; if Laura is Flora when young, Charity Finch is Flora as she would like to have been as an adult, able to share her love of learning and literature with the young.

Like all Flora's other books, *Still Glides the Stream* is full of keenly observed portraits of women, from Lady Louisa who rode to hounds at eighty, to the poorer neighbours:

> ... women who also knew how to do the right thing in their lesser degree. Learned only in country lore and Holy Scriptures, but keenly intelligent, they ruled over their families, fulfilled their personal obligations and used their spare energy in helping their neighbours. Racy of tongue, forthright in manner, firm believers in the cakes-and-ale side of life, with big comfortable bosoms and fat sides often shaken with laughter, they slapped life into the newly born and sped the dying with words of homely comfort. Their day has passed but in their day they served their

world well. In the family vault and the unmarked grave, peace be
to their ashes.[23]

The book had illustrations by Lynton Lamb, newly returned
from his war service but because of the economies still in force,
the pictures were only brief chapter headings.

Still Glides the Stream ends with the sentence: 'As she trod the
old footpath way with the sound of running water in her ears,
these thoughts gave her an extraordinary sense of comfort and
reassurance.' Comfort and reassurance were in short supply in
the era of the atomic bomb and it was unfortunate that the book
took so long to be published.

Flora was beginning to earn quite large sums in royalties, in
November 1946 the Reprint Society proposed to produce
15,000 copies of *Lark Rise to Candleford* which Geoffrey
Cumberlege thought might amount to £1,800, what he called,
'A little golden apple beginning to ripen'.

At about this time Flora bought another property in Brixham,
number 32 Bolton Street. It is a large, double-fronted house in
the centre of the town and was once a small hotel. John was still
buying and renting property but this one was kept as an
investment.

When Leslie stayed with Flora and John again that summer
she told him that she would like to have a ticket for the Irish
Sweep and he managed to get one for her. Later a telegram
from Dublin raised her hopes high, she had drawn the favourite,
Flag Wallah. In the end the horse finished fourth, so Flora did
not win the hoped-for fortune for her family but she had already
sold part of the ticket for £250 so she was quite pleased. She
wrote to Leslie, 'So our dear little horse did not win, I wish he
had for your sake and Basil's and Di's ... I am sending you £100
with our love, hoping it will help a little towards your heart's
desire.'[24]

John was so interested in this venture that he began to sell
sweepstake tickets, Flora teased him that he was getting to be
quite a sporting character.

After the war Flora was still finding books to add to Geoffrey
Cumberlege's collection, despite his admission that he was
expending his substance in: 'Riotous book buying,' which led to
his being ' ... perplexed daily by the problem of where to put my
books which overflow my shelves and swirl about me like a

Mississippi flood ... I long ago filled every nook and cranny at home, and I am very rapidly exhausting every inch of space in my office.'[25] Flora had been able to buy herself some books with the money she made from her writing over the years but now that she could afford more books her eyesight was too poor to read small print. As early as 1944 she had written to Mr Cumberlege that an edition of one of Thackeray's books was, 'too small for my present limited eyesight, very disappointing'.[26] But her pleasure in buying books for her dear friend and publisher continued. She found him a copy of *Rosina* by Austin Dobson with Hugh Thompson's illustrations and she was searching her local bookshops for the *Highways and Byways* series for him.

On Armistice day Flora was well enough to go to the service of Remembrance at the war memorial in Dartmouth, where she laid a poppy wreath in Peter's memory. She thought of her brother Edwin too and was touched to hear later from her sister, that Leslie had taken a wreath to Cottisford's war memorial.

The weather that December was very cold, snow came early in what was to be the notorious arctic winter of 1947. Flora was soon kept indoors by the terrible weather which gripped even the normally mild West Country. She told her nephew in a letter that he would not recognize Brixham it was so frozen up and she expected to be housebound all over Christmas. In fact she was ill in bed again at Christmas and John cooked the Christmas dinner and did it beautifully although he too was feeling low.

Throughout the harsh and prolonged winter of 1947 Flora was working. She corrected the proofs of *Still Glides the Stream* and wrote an article on her life and work, for *Readers News*,[27] the magazine supplied to its members by the Readers Union. Readers Union had published an edition of *Lark Rise to Candleford* as a spring book for members. The article by Flora was to provide background to the book. She called the article 'A Country Child Taking Notes', and it was published in March 1947. In the article Flora wrote of her lifetime of writing:

> I never could remember in after life when I began to write but at seven years old I was penning letters to Santa Claus to be attached to my own and my brother's Christmas stockings and a little later I was running a family magazine. In 1912 I began to write for the press and from that time on, short stories, articles and verse of mine appeared in various periodicals. But it was not

until the 1920s that the idea took shape in my mind that a book about my old home might please readers. At that time from 1921 to 1928 I was contributing a series of nature and countrylife articles to one of the Catholic weeklies. During these years I received many kind letters of appreciation from readers, at home and overseas. From these letters I found that the feature most liked in the articles were the sketches of country life and characters, remembered from my childhood, and I determined that in some future time I would describe them more fully.[28]

When the snows melted in March Brixham had terrific floods. Flora described what happened in a letter to Mrs Tylor.

The road outside our gate was a raging torrent like a river in spate. At the town end of the road the houses were flooded on the ground floors, the Post Office and most of the shops were awash and people in the lower part of the town had to be rescued from their upper windows by men in boats. Our cellar was flooded and we were without gas for twenty four hours. We have had five bursts of the pipes indoors and are still waiting for the plumber.[29]

All these troubles sapped her failing strength although she was out for walks again as soon as the sun shone.

Geoffrey Cumberlege's son Patrick had become a naval cadet and in 1947 he was at the Royal Naval College in Dartmouth. Before he left home Patrick Cumberlege was given Flora's address. He took a bicycle with him to Dartmouth and hoped to be able to cycle over to Brixham to see the Thompsons who had, through his father, invited him to Lauriston.

In the spring of 1947 he and a friend from the Naval College, went over to Brixham for Sunday tea on a number of occasions. Flora fed the young naval cadets cakes and clotted cream, although rationing was still in force and she herself was far from well. The fourteen-year-old naval cadet found her quiet but welcoming in the dark front parlour of Lauriston. The visits were hardly exciting and having just read her books, Patrick Cumberlege was rather disappointed at Flora's unwillingness to talk about her early life. At fourteen he cannot have realized how tired she was.

Early in the spring Flora wrote to tell her youngest sister of her illness during the winter, 'In some ways I was lucky,' she wrote, 'as I was in bed through the frost and snow. Poor little dead birds littered our garden.' She went on to say, 'my new book is still being held up at the printers on account of labour and other troubles but if all goes well it will be out sometime this year.' She signed her letter, 'ever your loving sister Flora-Floss-Flo-Floie, I answer to either.'[30] Her gentle humour never deserted her, although her strength was failing fast.

In May when the weather was warmer she seemed better and John felt happy to leave her on her own again when he went out for a day on business. When he came home in the evening, he did not find Flora downstairs and there was no meal prepared. He rushed upstairs to find her in bed again. She had had an attack of angina at midday. John sat with her until nearly eight when he went down stairs to make tea which he took up to her. He left her feeling better and more cheerful but at 9.45 when he went upstairs to go to bed himself he found Flora dead. She had had a heart attack. It was the swift and silent death of one who had lived quietly whilst giving joy to many.

17 Postscript

Flora was cremated following a funeral service in her old church, St Barnabas in Dartmouth. Her ashes were interred in Longcross Cemetery, Dartmouth. The granite headstone, shaped like an open book, has her name on one leaf, on the other, as instructed in her will, is the name of her beloved younger son Peter. The grave is tucked into a corner of the large municipal cemetery. The only headstones close to it are those commemorating Dartmouth sailors lost at sea during the war like Peter; Flora would not have minded their company and she would have liked her quiet corner. She would have been proud too, to see Peter's name remembered twice more in Dartmouth. His name is on the town's main war memorial in Royal Avenue Gardens, and in St Petrox Church, where his name appears with the list of service men and civilians of Dartmouth who died in the Second World War. Their names are inscribed on woodwork taken from an old gallery and placed beneath the west window. It would have pleased Flora that Peter's name should be remembered in that sturdy church built on a rock at the harbour mouth.

Amongst the obituaries which appeared when Flora died, one said, 'Those who were privileged to enjoy her friendship and her letters will not soon forget this quiet, witty and most kind of ladies.'[1]

Flora wrote her own memorial. Everything she was is contained in her writing, the elegies in her books are her own. She did, in the end fulfil the fortune told to Laura by the gipsy at Candleford Green, 'You are going to be loved by people you have never seen.'[2]

John Thompson never got over his wife's death. She would have been surprised at the effect it had on him, he was far more dependent on her than either of them knew. She was a strong, free spirit with intelligence and talent far greater than he possessed, without her he was diminished. At first he went back to Bournemouth to stay with friends, feeling stunned and ill. Later he went to the Isle of Wight and spent time with one of his sisters who ran a small hotel. When he returned to Devon he found Lauriston too large and lonely, he sold it and moved to another address in Brixham. He died there on 13 July 1948, he had survived Flora by only fourteen months.

Flora's last book *Still Glides the Stream* was not published until 1948. Her daughter writing to an admirer of her mother's work said, 'I feel so grieved she will never see the new book.'[3] The book was well received, reviews spoke of its 'lucid workmanship' and 'happy descriptive touches,'[4] but it did not get the acclaim which greeted her other books.

Winifred became her mother's literary executor carrying out her responsibilities very well. Soon after Flora's death she wrote to Geoffrey Cumberlege about the possibility of turning 'The Peverel Papers' into a book, an idea which Flora herself had wanted to carry out. Mr Cumberlege was interested, 'I think she was remarkably good at describing nature and she obviously had a deep knowledge of the subject,' he wrote, 'I should therefore be very favourably inclined towards this work of hers.'[5] But once again the project was not pursued.

Also amongst her mother's papers Winifred found the typescript of *Gates of Eden* which she sent to Oxford University Press. It was read by Geoffrey Cumberlege and other readers, none of whom liked it. This put Geoffrey Cumberlege in a difficult position, but he handled the rejection with characteristic tact, writing to the bereaved Winifred, 'It has charm but is distinctly dated, though I can well imagine that in fifty years' time from now it might be published for the first time as a discovery.'[6]

Unfortunately time has not made *Gates of Eden* any more readable. Parts of it are interesting for their echoes of *Lark Rise* but the basic story is too sentimental and the characters unreal. Flora's preference for real places and people did not equip her to write fiction. *Gates of Eden* remains an experiment in writing full-length fiction which will probably never appear in print.

Not long after Flora's death, the author and biographer Margaret Lane went to Oxfordshire hoping to find enough material for a memorial article. She travelled with her friend Joan Hassall, the well-known wood engraver and friend of Julie Neild who had engraved the illustrations for the trilogy. Joan Hassall had introduced Margaret Lane to Flora's books and together they went in search of Lark Rise. Margaret Lane also contacted Winifred and went to see her and looked through all Flora's papers. The resulting essay was published in The *Cornhill* magazine[7] in January 1957 and later in Margaret Lane's volume of literary essays, *Purely For Pleasure* published by John Murray in 1959.

In 1949 ill health forced Winifred to give up the nursing home which she had run with two nursing colleagues in Cheltenham, she went to live in Bath with her two friends. She missed her mother acutely, their relationship had been a close one. She had lost her younger brother, her mother and her father all in the same decade, her only close relative was her brother Basil in Australia. Administering her mother's literary estate filled much of her time in her semi-retirement and kept her in touch with the literary world and those who had loved her mother's work. She replied to letters from admirers, and from publishers requesting permission to quote from the books. Quotations from Flora's books soon appeared in country anthologies, school textbooks and on radio broadcasts at home and abroad.

In the late 1950s Winifred was told by a number of people that her mother's old home at Juniper Hill had become a place of literary pilgrimage. She was not entirely sure that Flora would have approved, in a letter to a friend she wrote, 'She was an extremely modest and reserved person and would probably have been horrified at the idea of such publicity.'[8]

Winifred gave permission for the trilogy to be produced in large type by The National Library For The Blind, for use by partially sighted readers, an edition which would have pleased

Flora who had difficulty herself reading small print at the end of her life. New editions of the trilogy continued to be printed, including an edition in the World's Classics series.

Winifred also gave her blessing to the celebrations which took place in 1966, to mark the ninetieth anniversary of Flora's birth but she did not live to see the celebrations in May, when 400 people watched local school children perform scenes from *Lark Rise*, in the grounds of Cottisford House. Many of the parts were played by pupils of Flora's old school. She would have appreciated the irony of her work being performed at the Manor House where, as a school pupil she had been taken on the school treat to have tea in the servant's hall. Whereas Flora and her friends had marched in, two and two through the shrubbery paths to the back door, her successors were welcome at the front. Later that evening after a special evensong in the church where Flora worshipped, Lord David Cecil, Goldsmiths Professor of English at Oxford gave an informal lecture on *Lark Rise to Candleford* to an audience of 200 people in the Rectory Barn at Cottisford. Reading extracts from the book, he allowed Laura to give his audience glimpses of nineteenth- and early twentieth-century country life.

In 1976, the year of Flora's centenary, a small plaque was put up on the house which was the end house in *Lark Rise*. Flora's birthplace had been demolished so the house which featured in her books was chosen to commemorate her life.

There were more celebrations in 1976 for the centenary. To mark this occasion there were events in Hampshire and Oxfordshire. A literary lunch was held at The Anchor inn at Liphook, attended by Sir Hugh Casson, Margaret Lane and Geoffrey Cumberlege. Later, in the afternoon Geoffrey Cumberlege opened an exhibition of Flora's life and times at the Selborne bookshop. The bookshop, which was once a Post Office, specialized in country books and its owner, Anne Mallinson mounted an exhibition of Flora's letters and manuscripts.

In Oxfordshire, Shelswell Park was the setting for the Lark Rise Festival, the same park had been the setting for Queen Victoria's Golden Jubilee celebrations which Flora and most of the hamlet families had enjoyed. For Queen Victoria there was tea in a marquee, taken one parish at a time, sports and a fair. For Flora's day, 1,500 people went to Shelswell Park to watch a gymkhana, a country dancing display, a fancy dress competition in which there were one or two 'Laura's'; there was a gipsy telling fortunes, bowling for a pig, horse and driving displays, all events which Flora would have recognized. Only one display would have surprised her, an exhibition of her own papers, photographs and books; even her typewriter was on display and a member of her family signed copies of her books. At the jubilee[9] young Laura, who hated crowds and noise, longed to escape to the shady woods and spinneys of the park. Flora might have felt the same if she had seen the crowd gathered to honour her memory eighty-nine years later.

Flora's unpublished work was not forgotten. Margaret Lane, who had looked through it in the late 1940s, decided to edit the unpublished sequel to the trilogy, which Flora had called *Heatherley*,[10] the account of her time in Grayshott. Although Flora had never offered it for publication, thirty years after her death there was enough interest in her life to make it worth publishing. *Heatherley* appeared with selections from 'Peverel Papers' and Margaret Lane's extended biographical essay as, *A Country Calendar* published in 1979.

Also produced in 1979 were two plays based on the trilogy, written by Keith Dewhurst. The first, *Lark Rise*, was staged at the National Theatre in 1978, the second, *Candleford Green* was first performed in 1979. The plays were so popular that *Lark Rise* was staged again in 1979, both plays being performed on the same day, one in the afternoon, one in the evening. The promenade style of the productions meant that the audience were involved in the scenes, of the first day of the harvest in *Lark Rise* and the day when the hunt met on the green, in *Candleford Green*.

Winifred did not live to see *A Country Calendar* published, nor the plays or the longer selection of her mother's nature essays published as *The Peverel Papers*[11] by Century Hutchinson in 1986. She had died in 1966, at Meysey Hampton in Gloucestershire. After her death, all her mother's papers were sent to the University of Texas. The publication of *The Peverel Papers* brought Flora's Hampshire essays to a much wider audience. The essays were her literary sketchbook and they give a clear picture of Flora's middle years and her maturing literary powers.

In a review of *The Peverel Papers* in the *Telegraph*[12] in 1986,

Richard Mabey spoke of Flora's willingness to expose her own vulnerability, without any support from the usual stereotypes of rural writing. It is this vulnerability, combined with what H.J. Massingham called her 'spiritual humility and exquisite reticence', which makes Flora and her work so well loved.[13]

At the end of her last book *Still Glides the Stream* Flora wrote:

> We come, we go, and, as individuals, we are forgotten. But the stream of human life goes on, ever changing, but ever the same, and as the stream is fed by well-springs hoarded by Nature, so the stream of humanity is fed by the accumulated wisdom, effort and hard-won experience of past generations.[14]

Flora's own life and hard-won experience enabled her to create books, lasting as the spirit of England and nourishing as the soil from which they sprang.

Notes

Abbreviations used in the notes

Works by Flora Thompson
ACC   *A Country Calendar*
CG   *Candleford Green*
BMP   *Bog Myrtle and Peat*
GOE   'Gates of Eden'
GTL   *Guide to Liphook, Bramshott & Neighbourhood*
HLY   *Heatherley*
LR   *Lark Rise*
LRTC   *Lark Rise to Candleford* (NB all chapter numbers refer to the trilogy)
OTC   *Over to Candleford*
PP   *Peverel Papers*
SGTS   *Still Glides the Stream*

Other
HJM   H.J. Massingham's introduction to *Lark Rise to Candleford*
HR   Flora Thompson papers held by the Harry Ransome Humanities Research Center, The University of Texas at Austen
ML   Essay on Flora Thompson by Margaret Lane (The *Cornhill*, 1957, No. 1011). Reprinted in M. Lane's *Purely for Pleasure*; expanded to form introduction to *A Country Calendar* (ed. M. Lane)
TCF   *The Catholic Fireside*
TLS   *The Times Literary Supplement*

1 Daughter of the Hamlet
1 Flora Thompson, *Lark Rise* (OUP, 1939), chapter 2.
2 Ibid.
3 Flora Thompson, *Over to Candleford* (OUP, 1941), chapter 18.
4 *LR*, chapter 11.
5 Presumably not kept by her. Known of through a reference in Flora Thompson's article in *Readers News* (Mar. 1947, Vol.9, No.10).

2 Growing Up
1 *LR*, chapter 1.
2 Henry David Thoreau, *A Writer's Journal 1840–1860* (Dover, p.22).
3 J.C. Bloomfield, *History of Cottisford, Hardwick & Tusmore* (J.W. Arrowsmith, Bristol, 1877).
4 *LR*.
5 Thomas Bewick, *A Memoir* (ed. Iain Bain, OUP, 1979).

6   William Barnes, *Poems of Rural Life* (Kegan Paul Trench, 1888).
7   Flora Thompson, unpublished novel, 'Gates of Eden'.
8   *LR*.

3   On Her Majesty's Service
1   Flora Thompson, *Candleford Green* (OUP, 1943), chapter 30.
2   Ibid.
3   Ibid.
4   Ibid.
5   *CG*, chapter 27.
6   *CG*, chapter 31.
7   *CG*, chapter 30.
8   Flora Thompson, short story, 'The Education of a Genius' (*The Ladies Companion*, 23 Nov. 1912)
9   *CG*, chapter 31.
10 Ibid.

4   Youthful Joys
1   *CG*, chapter 33.
2   Flora Thompson, *Heatherley* (published in *A Country Calendar* (ed. Margaret Lane, OUP, 1979)).
3   *CG*, chapter 33.
4   Alison Uttley, *A Country Hoard* (Faber & Faber, 1943).
5   *CG*, chapter 35.
6   *CG*, chapter 38.
7   Ibid.
8   *CG*, chapter 39.

5   Further Afield
1   *HLY*, chapter 1.
2   G.R. Pike, *Human Documents of the Lloyd George Era* (Allen & Unwin, 1972).
3   *HLY*, chapter 5.
4   Ibid.
5   *HLY*, chapter 3.
6   *HLY*, chapter 5.
7   *HLY*, chapter 8.
8   Ibid.

6   A Murder and a Mystery
1   *HLY*, chapter 10.
2   Flora Thompson, short story, 'The Nut Brown Maiden' (*The Ladies Companion*, 1913).
3   *HLY*, chapter 6.
4   *HLY*, chapter 11.
5   Essay by Margaret Lane (The *Cornhill*, 1957, No.1011); reprinted in *Purely For Pleasure* (John Murray, 1959); expanded to form introduction to *A Country Calendar* (ed. M. Lane, OUP, 1979).

7   Wife and Mother
1   Flora Thompson, essay, 'Skerryvore' (*The Catholic Fireside*, 5 June 1920, Vol. XVIII, No.1594).
2   ML.
3   Flora Thompson, 'The Silent Piano', cutting from an unidentified newspaper in the Harry Ransome Humanities Research Center, The University of Texas at Austen.
4   *HLY*, chapter 9.
5   *LR*, chapter 5.
6   *Peverel Papers* (*TCF*, Mar. 1924).
7   Flora Thompson, 'Edmund', unpublished MS in HR.
8   *HLY*, chapter 9.

8   Kitchen-table Writer
1   *PP* (*TCF*, XI).
2   *CG*, chapter 32.
3   *The Ladies Companion* (25 Feb. 1911, p.349).
4   Flora Thompson, short story, 'His Lady of the Lilacs' (*The Ladies Companion*, 9 May 1914, Vol. XLIII, p.618).
5   GOE.
6   *The Ladies Companion* (22 July 1911).
7   Flora Thompson, short story, 'The Toft Cup' (*The Ladies Companion*, 6 Jan. 1912, Vol. XXXIX, No.996).
8   *LR*, chapter 5.
9   George Bourne, Change in the Village (Duckworth, 1912).

9   Watershed
1   *Literary Monthly* (issue not known), reprinted in *Collected Poems of Ronald Campbell Macfie* (Grant Richards & Humphrey Toulmin, London, 1929).
2   op. cit.
3   Flora Thompson, short story, 'The Leper' (*Literary Monthly*, p.132).
4   *PP* (*TCF*, Apr. 1924, p.435).
5   *HLY*, chapter 3.
6   *CG*, chapter 35.
7   *HLY*, chapter 11.

10   The Bright Day
1   Flora Thompson, *Guide to Liphook, Bramshott & Neighbourhood* (F. Williams, Liphook, Hants).
2   *HLY*, chapter 11.
3   Ibid.
4   Ibid.
5   *PP* (*TCF*, Sept. 1924, p.315).
6   HR.
7   HR.
8   Flora Thompson, short story, 'Skerryvore' (*TCF*, 5 June 1920, Vol. LXVIII).
9   Flora Thompson, short story, 'The Hermit's Yew' (*TCF*, 11 Sept. 1920).

10   Thoreau, op. cit.
11   *TCF* (Vol. LXXI, No. 1624).
12   Flora Thompson, collection of poems, *Bog Myrtle and Peat* (Phillip Allan & Co., May 1921).
13   *TCF* (7 May 1921, Vol LXXI).
14   *BMP*.
15   Ibid.
16   Ibid.
17   HR.
18   *PP* (*TCF*).
19   Letter in private collection.
20   *PP* (*TCF*, July 1924, p.63).
21   Ibid.
22   *LR*.

11   The Journalist
 1   *TCF* (Nov. 1924, p.483).
 2   *TCF* (Sept. 1925, p.237).
 3   *TCF* (Apr. 1924).
 4   *PP*.
 5   *PP* (*TCF*, Feb. 1925).
 6   *PP* (*TCF*, July 1927, p. 73).
 7   Unpublished letters to Mrs Christine Tylor, deposited recently by Richard Tylor at Exeter University.
 8   *GTL*.
 9   *ACC*.
10   *PP*.
11   Ibid. (*TCF*, 1924).
12   Ibid.
13   *LR*.
14   *PP*, No.2. (The first Peverel Papers were numbered one to twelve, later only the month appeared as a heading.)
15   *PP*.
16   Ibid.

12   Griggs Green
 1   Unpublished private letters.
 2   *PP*, No. 5 (*TCF*, 1922, p. 172).
 3   Unpublished private letters.
 4   *CG*, chapter 36.
 5   Unpublished private letters.
 6   Betty Timms, *Little Grey Men of the Moor* (Harrap, 1925).
 7   Myldrede Humble Smith *Girls of Chiltern Towers* (Blackie, 1932).
 8   *PP*.
 9   ML.
10   *PP*.
11   *PP* (*TCF*, July 1927).
12   *PP*.
13   *Peverel Society Book of Verse* (The Peverel Society, Dartmouth).

14 *TLS* (10 Oct. 1929).
15 *PP.*
16 *PP* (*TCF*, Dec. 1927)
17 *PP* (*TCF*, July 1923).
18 HR.
19 Mary Russell Mitford, *Our Village* (George Whittaker, 1824).
20 *PP* (*TCF*, Sept. 1925).

13 Back to the Beginning
 1 HR.
 2 *PP* (*TCF*, Aug. 1923, p.188).
 3 A number of unpublished stories by Flora Thompson are in MS at HR.
 4 *The Letters of Mary Russell Mitford* (Selected by R. Brimley Johnson, Bodley Head, 1924).
 5 *BMP.*
 6 Ronald Campbell Macfie, *The Faiths & Heresies of a Poet Scientist* (Williams Norgate, London, 1932).
 7 HR.
 8 *The Odes of Ronald Campbell Macfie* (Humphrey Toulmin, London, 1934).
 9 ML.
10 Ibid.
11 Ibid.
12 GOE.
13 *LR.*
14 GOE.
15 *LR*, chapter 5.
16 GOE.

14 Lark Rise
 1 *PP.*
 2 HR.
 3 *PP* (*TCF*, Nov. 1923, p. 541).
 4 Flora Thompson, short story, 'The Tail-less Fox' (*The Lady*, 3 Dec. 1936).
 5 Flora Thompson, essay, 'Old Queenie' (*The Lady*, 29 Apr. 1937).
 6 *LR.*
 7 Flora Thompson, article, *National Review* (Aug. 1937, Vol. 109, No.654).
 8 *LR.*
 9 Flora Thompson, article, *National Review* (May 1938, Vol. 110, No.663).
10 *LR.*
11 Ibid.
12 Flora Thompson, article, *National Review* (Aug. 1937, Vol. 109, No.654).
13 *LR.*
14 Ibid.
15 Ibid.
16 *OTC*, chapter 16.
17 Letter in HR.
18 Ibid.
19 *LR.*
20 Letter in HR.

21 Letter in private collection. Extracts have appeared in the *Bicester Advertiser* (20 May 1973).
22 George Mackie, *Lynton Lamb Illustrator* (Scolar Press, 1978).
23 Lynton Lamb, *County Town* (Eyre & Spottiswoode, 1950).
24 *LR*.
25 HR.
26 Ibid.
27 *Yorkshire Post* (29 March 1939, p.6).
28 *Time & Tide* (15 April 1939, p.479).
29 *The Sunday Times* (no date).
30 *TLS* (13 May 1939, p.278).
31 *Bicester Advertiser*, op. cit.
32 H.J. Massingham introduction to *Lark Rise to Candleford* (OUP, 1945).

15 War Time
 1 Unpublished private letters.
 2 *OTC*.
 3 Letter in HR.
 4 Flora Thompson, unpublished MS, 'Dashpers', in HR.
 5 Letter in HR.
 6 Ibid.
 7 *The Observer* (13 July 1941).
 8 *The Spectator* (22 Aug. 1941).
 9 *TLS* (12 July 1941).
10 Letter in HR.
11 Ibid.
12 HR.
13 Flora Thompson, *Candleford Green* (OUP, 1943).
14 *CG*, chapter 32.
15 *Bicester Advertiser*, op. cit.
16 *CG*, chapter 39.
17 *TLS* (13 Mar. 1943).
18 The *New York Times* (2 May 1943).
19 *Time & Tide* (13 Feb. 1943).
20 HJM.
21 Letter in HR.
22 Ibid.
23 Ibid.
24 Ibid.
25 Letters in private collection.
26 Ibid.
27 Ibid.
28 Ibid.
29 Letter in HR.
30 Ibid.
31 Letter in private collection.
32 Ibid.

16 The Open Book
 1 Letter in private collection.

2   Letter in HR.
3   Ibid.
4   Ibid.
5   Letter in private collection.
6   Ibid.
7   Ibid.
8   *Country Life* (4 May 1945).
9   Flora Thompson, *Still Glides the Stream* (OUP, 1948).
10 Letter in HR.
11 Tylor letters, Exeter University.
12 *LR.*
13 A.E. Housman, *Last Poems.*
14 Letter in private collection.
15 Tylor letters, Exeter University.
16 Letter in HR.
17 ML.
18 *The Periodical* (OUP, April 1946).
19 Letters in private collection.
20 Tylor letters, Exeter University.
21 Letter in HR.
22 *SGTS*, chapter 1.
23 *SGTS*, chapter 2.
24 Letter in private collection.
25 Letter in HR.
26 Ibid.
27 Flora Thompson, 'A Country Child Taking Notes' (*Readers News*, Readers Union, March 1947, Vol.9, No.10).
28 Ibid.
29 Tylor letters, Exeter University.
30 Letter in private collection.

17 Postscript
1   HR.
2   *CG*, chapter 35.
3   Letter in private collection.
4   *TLS* (22 May 1948).
5   HR.
6   Ibid.
7   The *Cornhill* (Spring 1957, No.1011).
8   Letter in private collection.
9   Queen Victoria's Golden Jubilee, 1887.
10 *HLY.*
11 *The Peverel Papers* (ed. Julian Shuckburgh, Century Hutchinson, 1986).
12 *The Daily Telegraph*, 1986.
13 HJM.
14 *SGTS.*

Bibliography

Flora Thompson: Works published in book form
Bog Myrtle and Peat (Phillip Allan & Co) 1921
Lark Rise (OUP) 1939
Over to Candleford (OUP) 1941
Candleford Green (OUP) 1943
Lark Rise to Candleford (OUP) 1945
Still Glides the Stream (OUP) 1948
Heatherley (in *A Country Calendar*, ed. M. Lane, OUP) 1979
A Country Calendar (ed. M. Lane, OUP) 1979
The Peverel Papers (Century Hutchinson) 1986

Bechinsale, R. and M., *The English Heartland* (Duckworth) 1980
Bourne, G., *Change in the Village* (Duckworth) 1912
Chamberlin, G.R., *Life in Wartime Britain* (Batsford) 1972
Clapinson, M., *Victorian and Edwardian Oxfordshire in Old Photographs* (Batsford) 1978
Daunton, M.J., *Royal Mail* (Athlone Press) 1985
Emery, F., The Oxfordshire Landscape (Hodder & Stoughton) 1974
Freeman, R., *Dartmouth, A History* (Harbour Books) 1983
Horn, P., *Labouring Life in the Victorian Countryside* (Alan Sutton) 1987
Kelly, T., *History of Public Libraries in Great Britain* (The Library Association) 1973
Macfie, R.C., *Collected Poems* (Richards & Toulmin) 1929
Mingay, *The Victorian Countryside*, Vol. 182 (Routlege & Kegan Paul) 1981
Mingay, *Rural Life in Victorian England* (Heinemann) 1977
Munford, W.A., *Penny Rate* (The Library Association) 1951
Nowell-Smith, S. (ed.) *Edwardian England* (Oxford University Press) 1964
Pike, G.R., *Human Documents of the Age of the Forsytes* (Allen & Unwin) 1969
Pike, G.R., *Human Documents of the Lloyd George Era* (Allen & Unwin) 1972
Quennell, P., *The Day Before Yesterday* (Dent) 1978
Read, D., *Edwardian England* (Harrap) 1972
Reeves, J. *Poems of Emily Dickinson* (Heineman) 1959
Robinson, H., *The British Post Office* (Greenwood (USA)) 1948
Scott, Sir W., *Complete Poems*
Somerville, G., (ed.) Harp Aeolian, *Commentaries on the Work of Lady*

Margaret Sackville (Burrow Press Ltd) 1953
Staff, F., *The Penny Post* (Lutterworth) 1964
Symonds, J., *Portrait of an Artist (Conan Doyle)* (André Deutsch) 1979
Tate, W.E., *The English Village Community and the Enclosure Movement* (Gollancz) 1967
Taylor, C., *Fields in the English Landscape* (Dent) 1950
White, C., *Women's Magazines 1878–1965* (Michael Joseph) 1975
Yarwood, D., *English Costume* (Batsford) 1961

Index